Dear Pitman Publishing Customer

IMPORTANT – Read This Now!

We are delighted to announce a special free service for all of our customers.

Simply complete this form and return it to the address overleaf to receive:

A Free Customer Newsletter

B Free Information Service

C Exclusive Customer Offers – which have included free software, videos and relevant products

D Opportunity to take part in product development sessions

E The chance for you to write about your own business experience and become one of our respected authors

Fill this in now and return it to us (no stamp needed in the UK) to join our customer information service.

Name: _____ Position: _____

Company/Organisation: _____

Address (including postcode): _____

_____ Country: _____

Telephone: _____ Fax: _____

Nature of business: _____

Title of book purchased: _____

Comments: _____

---------------------------- **Fold Here Then Staple** ----------------------------

We would be very grateful if you could answer these questions to help us with market research.

1 Where/How did you hear of this book?
- [ ] in a bookshop
- [ ] in a magazine/newspaper
(please state which):

_____

- [ ] information through the post
- [ ] recommendation from a colleague
- [ ] other (please state which):

_____

2 Which newspaper(s)/magazine(s) do you read regularly?:

_____

3 When buying a business book which factors influence you most?
(Please rank in order)
- [ ] recommendation from a colleague
- [ ] price
- [ ] content
- [ ] recommendation in a bookshop
- [ ] author
- [ ] publisher
- [ ] title
- [ ] other(s):

4 Is this book a
- [ ] personal purchase?
- [ ] company purchase?

5 Would you be prepared to spend a few minutes talking to our customer services staff to help with product development? YES/NO

PITMAN PUBLISHING

The Business Publisher

Written for managers competing in today's tough business world, our books will help you get the edge on competitors by showing you how to:

- increase quality, efficiency and productivity throughout your organisation
- use both proven and innovative management techniques
- improve the management skills of you and your staff
- implement winning customer strategies

In short they provide concise, practical information that you can use every day to improve the success of your business.

FINANCIAL TIMES

PITMAN PUBLISHING

the Institute of Management

F O U N D A T I O N

PITMAN PUBLISHING

COMMUNICATE
TO WIN

COMMUNICATE TO WIN

12 Key Points for Success

Heinz Goldmann

FT
PITMAN
PUBLISHING

PITMAN PUBLISHING
128 Long Acre, London WC2E 9AN

A Division of Pearson Professional Limited

First published in Great Britain 1995

British Library Cataloguing in Publication Data
A CIP catalogue record for this book can be obtained
from the British Library.

ISBN 0 273 60848 7

1 3 5 7 9 10 8 6 4 2

Typeset by Northern Phototypesetting Co. Ltd., Bolton
Printed and bound in Great Britain by
Biddles Ltd, Guildford and King's Lynn

*The Publishers' policy is to use paper manufactured
from sustainable forests.*

It is vital for the success of our companies that businessmen and women emerge as real leaders and demonstrate their ability to communicate effectively, internally and externally.

Sir Colin Marshall, Chairman, British Airways Plc

CONTENTS

INTRODUCTION

COMMUNICATE – BUT HOW?

You will have picked up this book because you want to improve your ability to persuade others through communication. To put it simply: you would like to become a better speaker or, perhaps, you are an experienced manager who already knows how to speak well, but you would like to become outstanding, in the true sense of the word. That is by no means easy.

You're in good company. An American survey shows that most people are more afraid of giving a difficult speech than of becoming ill or disabled, being sacked or mugged, or suffering loss of money or property.

I can fully sympathize with the way you may feel before and after giving a speech. During my first few 'performances', the listeners walked out on me in droves. At the end of my first series of seminars – a total of 12 evenings – only a quarter of the original participants remained. No applause. No thanks. During the discussions afterwards, there was an embarrassing silence. No positive feedback whatsoever. Not a friendly word. The end was as depressing as the beginning. I am sure you are in a better position than that – it could hardly be any worse.

So, how was I able to turn these failures into successes? Perhaps you wish there could be some sort of a miracle cure. But there isn't – only patient, persistent hard work and the insights you will discover on the following pages. One person's experience, however, is certainly not enough proof of lasting success. My colleagues and I have tested the guidelines, methods and techniques described in this book hundreds, even thousands of times during our international communication seminars, in German, English, French, Italian and Swedish, throughout Europe, in the USA, South America and the Far East. For over 40 years we have listened to and analysed hundreds of successful and less successful speeches given at all kinds of events. These were speeches given by entrepreneurs, top managers, politicians, media representatives, trade unionists, experts and ordinary people. During this research one thing became clear: you can no longer persuade anyone using conventional methods of rhetoric or public speaking. Techniques like these are outdated and worn out. Look at it this way: would you rely on a car, telephone, radio, drug or a typewriter that was produced in the 1920s?

One-way information in the form of a lecture, where every word is read from a script, with gung-ho remarks, self-satisfied thoughts and set phrases delivered to an impatient audience, won't win anyone over to your side any more. Communication is something entirely different. You know that (or at least you feel it). You probably also know that everyone is talking about communication these days. Any self-respecting business now has a communication director, communication department, communication policy, communication strategy, communication philosophy, communication culture or turns to a communication consultancy. All this, however, only serves to hide the truth: people *say* communication, but what they really *mean* is information, an informational monologue, not a two-way process. Communication, however, is something different; it is, above all, about understanding each other, but also about integration, participation, feedback, agreement and common ground – *that is* a two-way process. The result is a dialogue.

You may say that this is difficult to put into practice. In fact, it is simpler than conventional rhetoric. And the structure of this book makes it even easier for you.

First, look at the 12 key rules of successful communication, set out on page viii. These are followed by a list of the 12 most common mistakes people make and then practical guidelines, listed in abbreviated form. These will be discussed in detail in the corresponding individual chapters. There are 12 of them – a chapter for each key rule.

Of course, a book cannot replace a seminar, but its structure will make it easier for you to grasp the material and put it into practice. Each chapter starts with four questions and four case studies. You will find the answers and solutions to these by reading the chapter. This method, which has already proven itself in my book *How to Win Customers*, allows you to study the subject in a controlled way and offers simple training guidelines.

Here is one more tip before you start: if you really make an effort to understand other people, they will understand you as well. Listen to others, and they will listen to you. Try to grasp exactly what it is *they want* to gain and you will win them in return.

THE 12 KEY RULES OF SUCCESSFUL COMMUNICATION

These 12 rules will help you speak in public – that is, communicate well.

1 **Prepare much earlier and more thoroughly.**

2 **Control your means of expression.**

3 **Use your key qualities: empathy and projection.**

4 **Remember EMMA – expectations, mentality, motivation and attitudes of the participants.**

5 **Turn listeners into participants – achieve active participation through dialogue.**

6 **Find a captivating opening.**

7 **Choose a compelling close.**

8 **Pay close attention to organizational details.**

9 **Control your stage fright.**

10 **Distinguish between the three categories of speeches – occasion, information and effect speeches.**

11 **Control the discussion – handle tricky questions and attacks correctly.**

12 **Above all, motivate!**

UNSUCCESSFUL COMMUNICATION – THE 12 MOST COMMON MISTAKES

You will not be able to speak in public successfully – let alone communicate – if you make the following 12 mistakes:

1   **Preparing the wrong way, too late or not at all.**

2   **Using contrived rhetoric in speeches.**

3   **Failing to empathize with the audience, and lacking projection to create impact.**

4   **Misjudging the audience.**

5   **Delivering monologues.**

6   **Choosing a meaningless or standard opening.**

7   **Concluding with a trivial close or none at all.**

8   **Overlooking factors in the organization of the event.**

9   **Surrendering to stage fright.**

10   **Failing to distinguish between the three different types of speech – occasion, information and effect speeches.**

11   **Being unable to handle questions, verbal attacks and interruptions.**

12   **Boring your audience.**

THE MOST IMPORTANT POINTS IN A NUTSHELL

On the following pages you will find a synopsis of the most important points to remember. Each one is then discussed fully in the corresponding chapters of the book.

1 Prepare early and thoroughly

The vast majority of speakers begin their preparations far too late. Yet, a careful analysis of your audience is essential in order to fulfil the first prerequisite of communication: finding a common objective. Then, and only then, can you begin the process of gathering your material, select-ing and organizing it and mastering your presentation. Setting a simple but precise objective is essential if your speech is to be a success. Prac-tise your presentation by delivering the speech aloud to yourself sev-eral times. Sportspeople practise for every single competition, and you should do the same! Don't ever give a speech without preparation and rehearsal. Even when you are asked to give a spontaneous speech after dinner or in an informal setting, there are a few tricks you can use to give you enough time for a brief preparation.

2 Control your means of expression

Speakers who use stilted, old-fashioned formulae are not be able to per-suade any audience. Don't deliver a sermon and don't read your text from a script. Use a clear voice and simple language, maintain eye con-tact and natural, dynamic body language. And always remember to KISS when speaking: keep it short and simple. In addition, your presentation should be appealing. The way you present your speech accounts for up to 80 per cent of its success, while its content accounts for only 20 per cent. Pictures have more impact than words, so make use of audio-visual aids.

Above all, plan very carefully *how* to deliver your speech! *What* to say will then come much more easily.

3 Use empathy and projection

Show the audience that you can empathize with them ('You are in a difficult position, ladies and gentlemen') and demonstrate your charisma ('... but I can assure you that things will be looking up from now on!') to create an impact. The ability to empathize with your lis-teners and the way you project your personality are essential to becom-ing a true communicator. To achieve empathy, it is vital that you follow the 'five to one' rule. That means use the terms 'you' or 'us' five times more often than 'I'. 'We' and 'you' will open the hearts and minds of your audience. If you are able to show you understand others and express your message forcefully, then you will succeed in persuading people and winning them over to your side.

4 Remember EMMA

Communication is rhetoric turned on its head. What is essential is not what the *speaker* wants, but what the *participants* want. Communicating with the participants means finding a common denominator. Every speech must be tailor-made to suit the target audience. What do the participants want? What do they expect? How do they think? What is it that makes them tick? How familiar are they with your topic? If you stick to EMMA, the content of your speech will be accepted.

5 Turning listeners into participants

Genuine communication means turning listeners into participants. A speech in the form of a monologue won't elicit much more than a weary smile and mere politeness from your audience. Active participation (AP), however, ('Would you have done it in the same way?', 'Do you agree with me?') will achieve impact and provide real feedback. That means a dialogue with constant involvement instead of a monologue. Read the plentiful examples illustrating active participation in Chapter 5.

6 Finding a captivating opening

The first sentence is the second most important part of your whole speech, yet some speakers lose their participants during this sentence. An exciting, promising beginning gives you a flying start. One good formula is an IBP – an initial benefit promise – that is, mentioning what is going to come as a benefit to the listener. Don't use set phrases like 'Good evening, ladies and gentlemen', 'It gives me great pleasure ...', 'I am particularly pleased that so many of you could be with us today'. Try to find a start which makes your audience sit up and listen – and which motivates them!

7 Choosing a compelling close

Your last sentence is your most important one. A good conclusion can even save a bad speech, but a weak finish ruins a speech. There are various possibilities: a final benefit promise (FBP), a vision, a projection into the future, an ultimate appeal. Any of these is far better than thanking the participants (what for?), fishing for compliments ('I hope that you ...') or finishing without a real ending ('... well, that's it').

8 Pay close attention to organizational details

Think about *everything* – from the choice of room, seating, acoustics, lighting and quality of air, through to avoiding interruptions and, last but not least, the breaks and possible refreshments. Organizational deficiencies, even minor things, can ruin your best speech. Even if these 'trifles' *don't* ruin your speech, they will still mar the impact you and your speech have on the audience.

9 Control your stage fright

Every really good speaker, whether TV presenter, politician or actor, has stage fright. Only those who don't care about their success or the impression they are making on others or have neither ambition nor drive can speak without feeling nervous. But that does not make them good communicators. Stage fright can stimulate and inspire you and mobilize your mental powers. If you manage to control your stage fright, you will be able to release your energy. Follow the ten helpful tips given in Chapter 9 to overcome tension.

10 Choose the right speech

Occasion speeches

Occasion speeches are given to entertain the listeners (after-dinner speeches), during celebrations (jubilees, inaugurations, etc.), or speeches to introduce or thank a speaker or to open and conclude an event.

It is important to tailor the speech to the occasion, its aim and methods used. An occasion speech should last no more than three to four minutes. Make frequent use of active participation (AP) and audiovisual aids, and illustrate with anecdotes, examples or quotes. Presentation is much more important than the actual content.

Information speeches

The aim of information speeches is to convey knowledge. Use AP and audio-visual aids continuously to facilitate understanding. Its duration should be a maximum of 20 minutes. Present data with visuals and check that the information is understood. Include frequent summaries, arouse curiosity and emphasize the benefits for the participants. And, above all, *MOTIVATE!*

Effect speeches

If you are not able to create real interest in the information you are conveying, you might as well save your breath. Effect speeches can be subdivided into the following types.

1 **Persuasion speeches:** influence opinions, presenting proposals and projects, 'sell' your ideas and suggestions during meetings, sales presentations etc.
2 **Motivation speeches** to motivate, create enthusiasm, pep talks, appeal to the listeners' ambitions, create positive feelings or reinforce a common goal.
3 **Action speeches** to achieve acceptance at board meetings, create a common view at company briefings, obtain decisions in committee meetings, launch a specific action.

As the target audience has a different attitude in each case (negative in 1, positive in 2 and committed in 3), the structure of your communication also has to be different. *Persuasion* speeches influence, convert and sell. *Motivation* speeches are intended to spark enthusiasm, encourage, motivate, whereas *action* speeches trigger controllable and specific immediate action.

11 Handling tricky questions and attacks properly

Speakers who give a good speech, but perform badly in the discussion afterwards often lose the entire impact of their presentation. In Chapter 13 you will find 12 tips and a series of tactical tricks that provide you with a helping hand. You should prepare each discussion carefully, you should also prepare for any attacks and criticism that might follow. Remember, above all, do not overreact. You want to win people, not battles.

12 Above all, motivate!

There are two aspects to motivation. First, you need to appeal to the participants' primary motives and desires, such as prestige and security, or touch on other goals in life, for example, personal development, success, performance, career, affection, friendship, happiness, health or quest for knowledge. Appealing to these key concepts will help you win friends and persuade them.

Second, you have to hold the attention of your audience throughout by involving them – in short, motivate them to listen to you. If you fail to achieve this, your speech will have no effect. Even when communicating bad news (lay-offs, bad business results) you have to motivate your listener(s) with the help of commitment, positive ideas, suggestions, possible solutions or future improvements. Remember: a good motivator appeals to the heart, not to the mind.

If you follow the advice given in these 14 chapters, you will be able to win over others, whether colleagues, customers and possible clients, superiors, partners, friends or even opponents – by means of communication. Communicate to win!

Heinz Goldmann
Geneva, September 1994

1

PREPARE EARLY AND THOROUGHLY

Can you answer the following four questions?

1 Will you remember your speech better if you prepare it at the very last minute?

2 Is it true that it takes twice as long to prepare a speech than to deliver the finished version?

3 Is it possible, if necessary, to ask an assistant to collect and organize the information you need for the speech?

4 Is it better to be the first speaker at an event or the last?

Can you solve the following four problems?

1 Paul Smith is a famous advertising expert. His agency is flourishing. He is often being asked to talk about his work and present his ideas. Paul has considerable experience in public speaking. He always tells the exciting story (exciting for him at least) of how he founded his agency; then goes on to present his very successful advertising campaigns of the last few years, interspersed, as always, with the same witty remarks. As he is prone to forgetting facts and figures, he reads most of his speech from a script. The reactions to his speeches are quite positive. Paul Smith comes across as a congenial person, but he is beginning to wonder why he fails to win more new clients even though his presentations are well attended.

Do you know why? What should he do differently?

_____

_____

_____

2 Brian Milligan, Manager of a data processing company, is a brilliant speaker. He not only knows his subject extremely well, he also knows how to grab his audience with exciting stories and always finds exactly the right tone. And he talks without a script. But, somehow, Brian Milligan often ends up drifting off the subject: he chats away, loses his thread, forgets important illustrations he has prepared and gets his slides mixed up.

What advice would you give him? What other problems could arise during his presentations?

_____

_____

_____

3 'I don't mind _when_ I talk', Dr Mary Steel, environmental expert in a large oil company, says to the organizer of an evening seminar on the subject of 'economy and ecology' and so it happens that she is almost the last one to speak. Before her allotted slot, speakers from political parties, environmental protection agencies and citizens' pressure groups give their presentations. By the time Dr Steel steps on to the platform, the participants have been sitting on their chairs for two hours and have listened to six speeches. Each speaker has gone over their allocated time by about five minutes. The participants are tired and hardly able to take anything else in. Dr Steel's prospects of successfully presenting her point of view, in spite of excellent material, are very slim.

Where has she gone wrong?

_____

_____

_____

4 A German businessman is invited for the first time to give a lecture in Spain. He is assured of competent translation. As usual, he prepares his speech carefully. Yet, once abroad, he is faced with completely new problems. He only realizes this a few hours before his presentation. The unforeseen difficulties make him lose his confidence and his lecture turns into a flop.

Which problems are being referred to here? What advice would you have given him for his preparation?

_____

_____

_____

EVERYDAY COMMUNICATION

A top executive's typical working week looks something like this:

Monday
Opening of a new factory. Speech to be given to the staff.

Tuesday
An important raw materials supplier has announced a visit for that day. This will entail complicated negotiations.

Wednesday

Board meeting. The members of the board expect a detailed report on the position of the company and suggestions for radical rationalization measures.

Thursday

A journalist from a leading business magazine has asked to interview you on the subject of the deteriorating results of the company during the first six months of its current financial year.

Friday

In the morning, there is a farewell speech and presentation for a departmental manager who is retiring. In the afternoon, the trade union representatives would like to discuss the threat of possible redundancies.

Speeches, meetings, lectures, differences of opinion, discussions, interviews, negotiations, debates – all of these are part of a top manager's everyday communication tasks. In spite of that – or perhaps as a result of that workload – they are trained either insufficiently or not at all. As a consequence, even experienced executives make a lot of mistakes when communicating. It is a difficult part of an executive's role, with the potential for mistakes to be made.

> **Don't leave it until the last minute to prepare for a speech!**

This is often countered with the argument: 'If I prepare a subject just before having to present it, I can remember it more easily during my speech.' Others argue: 'I don't have the necessary time to prepare thoroughly, so I write the whole speech down.'

Both arguments are wrong. Preparation takes time. But, the earlier you prepare, the less you have to do – your brain will work 'overtime' without your realizing it. If you don't have the time to prepare well in advance and thoroughly enough, give a shorter speech.

The following table should help you decide what to do.

Should I speak?

The ideal situation? 'A' speeches. 'C' speeches are to be discussed. The share? When 1A and 2A are matched by 3C!

Assessment criteria	Value		
	A	B	C
1 Obligation	unavoidable	limited	none
2 Impact	great	limited	small
3 Risk	low	medium	high

Here are two examples that illustrate how this table works.

1 The obligation in the case of an after-dinner speech is mostly minimal. Even when it is very successful, its effect is limited and the risk involved is usually medium.

2 On the other hand, in your capacity as chairperson of the Board, you have to speak at an annual general meeting. That is unavoidable. The impact can be great, but so is the risk. You can avoid the after-dinner speech, but you have to give the other – and give it well. The more often your value criteria (1 and 2) are located in the left-hand columns, the more thorough your preparation must be.

Before committing yourself to giving a speech, think very carefully whether or not you should really speak. A failure will leave scars, sometimes even open wounds. You are risking your own hide so make your decision accordingly. But, here is a word of warning on the basis of decades of experience: two-thirds of all unsuccessful speeches fail before the first word is even spoken due to lack of preparation.

PREPARATION

You must go through your material and absorb it thoroughly. This can't be done in five minutes, even if all you have to do is give a 15-minute routine talk to factory visitors. As a rule, preparation takes ten times longer than the speech itself. Yes, *ten* times! No professional speaker would do it any other way, so the same goes for you. Only the smallest part of your work will be seen – or rather heard – and that is your speech. It is the tip of the iceberg. The largest part of your work, the preparation, remains hidden from the participants. If you spend less time you take a risk – often an unjustifiable one. What you can cut down without any problems, however, is the length of your presentation. If you do this, you will do everyone a favour.

If you start your preparation too late, you will come under time pressure, a feeling of panic will set in and you will not be able to perform well on the day. There is no other way. Forget about reading from a script. That is the opposite of communication. It will isolate you from your audience and create additional tension. No-one would listen to you if you did, even if you think you can read extremely well. There are four stages in preparation:

1 researching
2 selecting
3 constructing
4 rehearsing.

Due to a lack of time, most people try to pack all four stages into one. That won't work, as they are all very different.

There are certain time-saving preparation techniques, but there is no way around careful preparation. Preparation is, in all cases, a 'maturing process', requiring time. Work on the four stages separately. Up until now, you have probably started your preparation with planning the content. At best, you may produce a reasonably good speech, but not true communication.

Stage 1: researching the material

Your first question during the *research* should be: *'What do the participants want and expect?* The second: *'What do I want?'* And the third: *'Where is the common denominator between me and them?* If you can't find a good answer to the last, you have a minimal chance of making a successful speech.

You must always start with the participants. *Only then* should you think about what you want to say and how. A careful analysis of the participants is essential in order to answer the first question. Who are they? Who will be coming? How receptive are they? What do they know? What do they want? (See also Chapter 4 on this point).

The answers to these questions will also help you to find the right tone. If you were to talk to a group of qualified doctors, you would treat the subject of sport at work differently than if you were talking to a group of apprentices. And 12 or 13-year-old pupils, who are dragged off on a 4-hour visit to a chemical plant by their teacher will be less receptive than a group of journalists visiting the site, who are making enquiries about the dangers involved in chemical production. (See Chapter 4 for more.)

Once you have worked out your ideas, bearing in mind the make-up of your audience, you should try to exhaust all available sources of information: friends, colleagues, experts, employees, literature, archives, to name but a few. There are more sources than you would initially believe. Have you gathered enough facts? Write *everything* down, without exception. Make lots of notes, but don't make any judgements yet. You will do that later. Otherwise, you will slow yourself down and may stop the creative process.

Stage 2: selecting

Now follows the selection and elimination process. *Only now* judge the quality of your material: good information goes into your script, the weak points go into the bin. Rate your points according to the following scale:

Types of points	Value
1 Main points – absolutely essential	5 points
2 Important subpoints – valuable	3 points
3 Further points – still useful	1 point
4 Padding material – keep in reserve, but most to be discarded	$\frac{1}{2}$ point
5 Uninteresting points or those irrelevant to the subject	0 points

Using this scale, you can judge the quality of your material. If you are not satisfied with the quality, seek out more material. Once you have gathered a large amount of information, mark each part with a 'B' (for beginning), an 'M' (for main body) or an 'E' (for end). In most cases, the largest quantity of notes will be marked 'M' and fewer – or none at all – 'B' and 'E'. Yet the beginning and the end are the most important parts. That is why the next step is absolutely essential: elimination. Anything that is superfluous should be thrown out. Mercilessly. Less is often more! Perhaps you have forgotten something? Your objective, perhaps? Your objective must be short, clear and consistent. Otherwise, you are asking too much of both the sender and receiver; you must do justice to both.

Stage 3: constructing

This is the time to construct your list of key words ('speech-guide'). There is a special technique using key words to help you speak freely. You work your way from key word to key word. The form below illustrates an example of this technique. On your version of this form, write down the main points, which you will use as landmarks to orientate yourself during the speech, and the subpoints, which are there to illustrate your main points. In the instructions column, put down all the instructions you want to give yourself – for example, when to show which overhead, which slide, which film clip, when to raise your voice or when to involve the participants. You should work this out accurately in advance. In the far left column, put down the time allocated to the individual parts of your speech and, to the right of it, a cumulative total. Here is a good tip.

> **Phrase the opening and the close of your speech word for word and learn them by heart! Three sentences each, no more.**

These two most important parts of your speech must be memorized particularly well (see Chapters 6 and 7 for more on this).

Practise moving from one point to the next!

This will enable you to talk freely. Use the key words as landmarks and practise moving between them.

Speech-guide

Time in minutes		Instructions	Headings – key words	Reserve points
Part	Total	to yourself		Examples
I	I	Eye-contact	Opening (word for word)	
3	4	OHP1	I	
8	12	Slide 1	2	
2	14	AP1 (...)	3	
10	24	Video 1	4	
2	26	AP2 (...)	5	
5	31	Tape 1	Poss. 6	Poss. 6
2	33	AP3 (...)	7	
5	38	OHP2	8	
2	40	Loud, slow	close (word for word)	

Key:
AP = active participation
poss. = could possibly be left out (lack of time, etc)

Stage 4: rehearsing

Rehearsing is the fourth stage of your preparation. Present your speech before the event once, twice or even three times to a colleague, a test group, your secretary or your partner. If this is not possible, taping or video-recording yourself is a useful way to check your performance.

Practise the trial run as if it were the real thing: go through everything exactly as you would at the event, putting the transparencies on the overhead projector and talking through each point as it occurs. Practise AP, even down to the handing over of a gift at a retirement party and the few words you will say. The more often you rehearse and also take into account the feedback given by your guinea pigs, the better you will perform when it really counts.

You could enlist the help of someone else to collect the material, for example your secretary or a colleague. But selecting and developing your material has to be done by you. The fine-tuning cannot be delegated to anybody else and no-one can rehearse for you, nor, for that matter, give the speech. Otherwise you would be better off leaving the presentation entirely to someone else. If you decide to speak, do it properly. Only you know what really matters.

It is not possible to copy speeches or even phrases from textbooks either. They will never be 'yours'. And don't try to imitate 'perfect' speakers; it will not work. The participants – and you – will notice immediately that you are stiff and stilted, and are trying to be someone other than yourself! That is why pre-prepared speeches that have been used by somebody else, even if they were successful, won't work for you.

> **Remain yourself – use your language, your ideas, your experience, your examples and your own personality!**

Good preparation also includes time planning. Almost all speeches are too long and would be better if the material was simply cut by a third. Audiences tire very quickly. If you try to give something for everyone, you will end up giving nothing for anyone.

Most speakers do not communicate, they deliver monologues. They do not establish an on-going contact with their audience. Neither do they turn listeners into participants by including active participation (AP) or involvement. That is outdated rhetoric, not communication. You will learn more about the techniques involved in achieving true communication later.

SOME OTHER IMPORTANT POINTS

If you are one of several speakers, try to influence the sequence of the presentations. Whenever possible, be the first one to talk! And start with point one: your common goal. The last speaker has the most difficult job because much has been said before and often there is less time left than planned as the previous speakers will have overrun their time. The participants – if they are still sitting in their places at all – will be tired, impatient and restless. These are rather bad conditions for successful communication, so it is highly unlikely that your speech will go down well. For this reason, only in exceptional circumstances, and when you are absolutely certain of your success, should you agree to be the last to speak.

Should one never improvise? The answer is no. You'll risk a flop and you cannot afford that. Prepare! Even a few minutes' preparation is safer than none. Even if you are asked spontaneously at the dinner table to give a speech, you should never get up and speak immediately. You need time to think about what you would like to say. Postpone your speech until later in the proceedings, saying, for example, 'I would be delighted to say a few words; I think the best time would be after dinner'; or 'Allow me a few minutes to gather my thoughts together'. Or you could ask your neighbour to say a few words on the subject instead. Or you could simply decline the invitation to speak. Next time you will be prepared and won't be taken by surprise again.

In future, you will do things differently. Preparing well in advance and thoroughly is the first step on your way to success – success through communication. The whole process takes less time than you might think – you just need to plan and use your time more effectively.

> You should now have no trouble answering the four questions posed at the beginning of this chapter and solving the four communication problems.

Your speech is only the tip of the iceberg. The preparation behind it cannot be seen – but it can be felt. Approximately two-thirds of all unsuccessful speeches are not prepared properly. That is why you should always use the four-stage preparation process.

2

CONTROL YOUR MEANS
OF EXPRESSION

Can you answer the following four questions?

1 Can you establish eye contact even with a large group?

2 Is there any material in your speech that can be shortened?

3 What is the KISS formula?

4 Do you lose credibility when you present a complicated subject in a simple way?

Can you solve the following four problems?

1 Tim Jones believes that he cannot speak freely, so he writes his speech down word for word, learns it by heart and then tries to deliver it as if he were not reading it. He wonders why he doesn't feel very comfortable and his listeners hardly show any positive reactions, despite the fact that the content of his speech is technically 100 per cent perfect – so perfect it could be printed. As he is ambitious he intends to memorize his speech even better next time.

What advice would you give Tim?

_____

_____

_____

2 Dr Mary Higgins, product manager in an electronics company, and her colleague, Jacqui Richards, are both very confident. They speak on the same subject, with a similar content and are equally well prepared. And yet, the participants react completely differently to each of them.

What could be the reason for this?

_____

_____

_____

3 Two sales engineers, Tony Schwarzenberg (who has 15 years' professional experience) and Nigel Pilgrim (who has 5) have both been asked to talk to a group of customers about their products. Tony has prepared his speech very carefully, and before he starts he distributes handouts containing all the relevant information and data about the products. He asks the participants to save their questions until the end. His colleague, Nigel, whose speech is not nearly as informative as Tony's, regularly asks the participants questions during his speech, quotes figures and invites the participants to interpret them, and summarizes frequently (even obvious points).

One of them is clearly better received by the participants. Who is it? Why?

_____

_____

_____

_____

4 Terence Darby, a local government Administrator, has been a civil servant for 20 years. He has to report regularly to his superiors. He tries to make sure that there are no mistakes in his presentation, either in form or content. His language is as clear as crystal and his facts are absolutely correct. He comes across as knowledgeable and committed to his task. There is nothing to criticize about his report. His superiors consider him to be competent and ambitious, but slightly stiff and not really effective as a speaker. Consequently he is passed over for opportunities to speak in public.

But why? Terence has never made a mistake in his reports. Or is that not what counts?

_____

_____

_____

IT'S NOT WHAT YOU SAY ...

We all know speakers like this: Dr Richard Beech addresses his colleagues with a stiff and stilted presentation. He reels through phrase after phrase, saying things like 'Ladies and gentlemen, I am particularly delighted to have the opportunity to talk to you today ...', 'the time available is unfortunately not sufficient to ...', 'allow me to say the following before getting to the real subject', 'many of you undoubtedly know more than I do on the subject matter, but ...', 'the reasons for my presenting this topic are manifold, such as ...', 'I have given a lot of thought to the ways in which ...' and 'in any case I will do my best to keep my speech as brief as possible'.

The fact that his listeners (not even participants) are tired, not the least bit interested, and bored, is quite independent of *what* Dr Beech says. *It is the way he says it* that is wrong. He does not communicate with his participants, he gives a speech. None of his sentences are really natural. He does not establish eye contact, his voice is low, he comes across as being tired, disinterested and bored, although this might not really be the case. He shows no drive or energy, what he says 'does not go down well' and he arouses no positive reactions and feelings.

> **Emotions and feelings are more important than reason and logic.**

Eighty per cent of the impression you make depends on the way you present and barely 20% depends on the actual content. Most participants at a presentation are, however, not actively aware of this.

Dr Beech has not mastered all the instruments of expression at his disposal. He does not use his 'weapons', so he remains bland and his speech has no effect. And yet it is so easy to make a real impact on your participants. You only have to follow a few rules.

> **Stay natural, be yourself!**

Clichés are boring. Using them in a speech amounts to insulting the participants. A speaker who uses hackneyed expressions cannot or does not want to speak normally. A speech full of stilted phrases – even polite ones – cannot expect to get a positive response. A speaker who appears to be in a verbal strait-jacket, and uses trite and overworked phrases to begin and end a speech, will not be able to interest, move or touch an audience – let alone win them over (for more about good beginnings and endings see Chapters 6 and 7).

No better is the performance of chief executives who want to communicate information to their receptive staff and start their well-formulated, rational speech on the company's results with 'The last financial year shows a satisfactory development of the business' and end with a formal 'The Board would like to thank all members of staff and hope that our successful cooperation will continue to benefit our company'. In between – no involvement, no excitement, no commitment, no fun, no real gratitude – nothing but facts and figures.

Dr Beech has made yet more mistakes that are committed by almost all speakers. Can you spot them?

Establish a rapport with the participants!

If you succeed in establishing a rapport you will have already achieved the first aim of communication. People will see you as a nice person. This is the most important preliminary as it enables you to achieve the second aim: winning people over. And the third is persuading people. But *how* do you establish a rapport?

Try KISS next time: keep it short and simple. Almost all speeches are far too long and expect too much from the audience. So, simply leave out a third of your material – and, instead, explain your arguments better. And simplify what you are going to say. Real experts convey complicated matters in easy terms. Only incompetent people make simple things sound complicated. Clear, simple language helps the participants listen more easily. Avoid anything that is reminiscent of jargon. Make it shorter and simpler!

It is so simple

The Lord's Prayer consists of 57 words, the 10 Commandments of 297 words and the American Declaration of Independence 300 words – while the European Union Regulation on importing caramel products has 26 911 words.

Really important statements *can* be expressed in a few words if you get to the point more quickly. Beating about the bush for too long makes you lose your participants and many speakers lose themselves – and their listeners – in sentences that are far too long.

Here are some general rules on sentence length.

- **Sentences of up to 10 words are easily comprehensible.**
- **Sentences of up to 16 words are comprehensible.**
- **Sentences of up to 22 words are still comprehensible.**

- **Sentences with more than 22 words are no longer comprehensible.**

Here are some general rules on sentence length.

Less is often more. If you manage to say in 15 minutes what takes others 30, you are twice as effective as they are. Arouse curiosity. Turn your listeners into real participants by asking them questions, inviting comments and even leading the participants to draw conclusions jointly. This will make your communication more interesting.

A mistake that is typically made by top managers – and politicians – but by no means by them alone, is that they try to give too much detail. They try to include in the speech something of interest for every single participant. No one should feel ignored, everyone should feel included, but this habit can have serious consequences:

> **Those who try to offer something for everyone end up giving nothing to anyone.**

An example of good communication

An exporter I know used to say to representatives of the chamber of commerce: 'We need to increase our exports to south-east Asia, which gives rise to the question to what extent this is possible today and what solutions present themselves.' Today he says the same thing, but more shrewdly: 'Can we increase our exports to south-east Asia? That is the question! And how do we go about it? Any ideas?' Create suspense! Again, make it shorter and simpler.

> **Put question marks and exclamation marks into your speech.**

ILLUSTRATE YOUR SPEECH!

An example or a striking comparison is worth more than ten minutes of theoretical explanations. A sales director wants to illustrate to the sales force how many customers the company has lost over the last year. He does not simply mention the figure 600, but illustrates it by using a comparison. 'There are 60 people in this room. Imagine every one of you is a customer. Now have a look at everybody in this room!' He gives his colleagues a moment to reflect on this. Then he goes on to say, 'Right, that makes 60 customers. And we have lost 10 times that number. That means 10 per cent of our clients and more than ten per cent of our turnover. A drain which our company cannot put up with in the long run. So ...'

Here are a few simple hints:

1 Examples

Try it. Say, 'For example, we could do the following ...' or, 'For example, it so happens that ...' or, 'For example, the solution could achieve ...'. You will see how attentively the audience will follow your words. As examples are concrete illustration tools, they create understanding much earlier.

2 Episodes

These are, for example, events taken from everyday (working) life, which are easily remembered or those that remind us of our joint experiences. 'You know, when we had the fire, John ...' or 'Talking of customer service, the other day I had a call from a customer at a quarter to eight. Do you know what he wanted?'.

3 Anecdotes

Short stories, anecdotes and jokes related to the subject matter not only help to loosen up the presentation, they can also illustrate certain points in an entertaining way.

So remember, integrate examples and episodes – anything that helps the participants to follow you. Use them to create suspense and help easy understanding.

Audio-visual aids

The same is true for audio-visual aids. Things you see are retained seven times better in your memory than things you hear! Participants lose their receptiveness far quicker than you would believe, especially if they only have things to listen to and nothing to see. This is why you should illustrate your speech with pictures, drawings and charts. One per minute is a good average. Keep your participants' eyes busy, for the following reason.

> **If the eyes are opened, the ears will open as well!**

There are numerous simple ways of doing this. For example, you can be more daring and creative in the use of your visual aids. Generally speaking, though, they can't be *too* original. Sales manager John Britain, speaking about his company's sluggish sales in South America, uncovers a map behind him and on the table in front of him he places a couple of bananas, coconuts and some coffee from Brazil. As he says 'Our customers in Brazil will be jumping for joy to hear that they will only have to pay 80 per cent of the current price from now on', he shows a photo of laughing Brazilian youths on the beach at Copacabana. At the end of his speech, John says: 'Our new promotional aids will be welcomed enthusiastically by our Brazilian dealers.' At the same time, he plays a video clip showing 100 000 cheering fans in the football stadium at Rio de Janeiro.

Even the driest subject can be livened up and presented in an interesting way with the help of visual or audio-visual aids. If you were giving a presentation on the Chinese imperial dynasties, you might bring a little Chinese vase along – or a flute or a handful of rice. During your speech, say 'Can anyone guess what I have here?' You are bound to hold everyone's attention.

The classic example of a spectacular audio-visual effect was Khrushchev's appearance at the UN. When the Soviet party chief, seemingly excited, banged his shoe on the desk to emphasize his point, people were startled and many listeners believed they were witnessing a spontaneous act. But they were wrong. This spectacular performance had been planned – as is proven by a photo showing Khrushchev from behind: neither of his feet are without a shoe, and in his hand he is holding a third – the famous – shoe. That was in 1960 and even today people remember it. Also, think about the public appearances made by Gandhi, John F. Kennedy, Ronald Reagan, Pope John Paul II and Fidel Castro. They were, and are, all masters of visualizing messages.

> **Be creative!**

Audio-visual aids should be spectacular, but they also have to be clear and comprehensible. Do not distribute hard copies of your speech beforehand, do not use more than 20 words per overhead transparency. Use, at the most, two images and everything you use must be legible and visible.

Other visual aids

Other important aids are your use of expression, body language and eye contact to make an impact.

Expression

This means voice and language. Your voice is your business card. A voice that is too soft and gentle lulls the audience to sleep. So does a monotonous, boring voice. The ideal is a strong, clear and striking voice – a voice that is charismatic. A good tactic is to be very strong at the beginning of a sentence, and at the end. Vary your tone but never drop your voice at the end. Always stress the end syllables and give a special emphasis to the end of each sentence. And the language? It has to be as clear and simple as possible – use language that every participant will understand, that neither obscures nor assumes too much knowledge on the part of the participants. And, as we have seen, keep the sentences short. To use a marketing phrase: make it easy to buy from you.

Body language

This encompasses your facial expression, body position, vigour and liveliness, which all have an effect on your participants. If you stand or, worse, sit behind a desk, bent over, with arms folded and no expression on your face, you will hardly have a positive impact on the participants. However, you will create a pleasant atmosphere if you stand directly in front of the group (as short a distance away as possible), are active, emphasize your words, look around in a friendly way, and smile now and then. Top managers often have difficulty with this – they 'shrink' as if they were weighed down by a heavy load, looking stern, too controlled and uninvolved. Body language betrays attitude, confidence and mood – both positive and negative.

Eye contact

This is indispensable. Look away and your audience will look away. Look at your audience and they will look at you. Anyone can do that! Mobilize your charisma and a certain amount of willpower. You should be in control. Make this clear to your participants. Look at them with confidence. This will help you notice whether – and how – the participants look at you. This gives you the necessary feedback and self-confidence and reinforces your impact. Eye contact can be used with large groups as well. Let your eye wander from one part of the audience to the next. Don't ever let it rest on one person alone!

> **Expression, body language and eye contact are powerful tools. Use them consistently for triple impact.**

Have you mastered these tools? If you are not sure, test yourself with a video camera. Alternatively, ask a couple of friends to listen to you, while you practise your expression (voice and language), body language and eye contact. Ask your friends how they think you are performing. And, as always, practical experience is far better than theory. It is not enough just to read this book. You have to *use* what you have learned, and this can only be done through practise, practise and yet more practise …

Being liked

A world-famous German chief executive once gave a presentation to several hundreds of his French colleagues. He was particularly pleased about the warm, friendly response to his very informative presentation, as he had practised the contents, as well as the French intonation and expression very carefully. When he asked what had specifically impressed the participants, the answer came as a surprise to him: his smile, charm, elegance and wit – not the sophisticated content of his speech. Go and try it for yourself! Win the heart and the head will follow.

> **No doubt you will now be able to answer the four introductory questions and solve the four case studies!**

Make your communication task easier for yourself! You will achieve better understanding by expressing yourself simply and with conviction. Experts can present complicated facts in a simple way. Remember to use KISS. Make constant use of visual aids, expression, body language and eye contact. Make people feel that you are a nice person.

3

USE EMPATHY AND PROJECTION

Can you answer the following four questions?

1 Can empathy and charisma be learned? Can one of these qualities replace the other?

2 What does the 5:1 rule mean?

3 Can the participants be expected to make an effort to tune into the speaker as well or is it only the speaker who has to tune in to his participants?

4 Why is it that top executives are often worse speakers than their lower-ranking colleagues?

Can you solve the following four problems?

1 A large international hotel chain is looking for a new head of public relations, a position that reports directly to the Board. Two women have been short-listed for the job. Both applicants have similar qualities. However, there is one thing on which they differ substantially.

During her interview, Applicant A makes detailed enquiries about the general problems of the company and, in particular, problems that the PR Department is faced with. She asks where bottlenecks have occurred in the past and how colleagues get on with each other. She displays considerable interest in the internal circumstances of the company to the Director of Personnel.

Applicant B tries specifically and forcefully to convince the Director of Personnel of her qualities. She describes her past positions and emphasizes her considerable experience.

After the interviews, both applicants are asked to support their applications with a brief presentation to the members of the Board.

Which applicant do you think will perform better in the presentation?

_____

_____

_____

2 'I want to increase our turnover by 20 per cent in the coming year. That is bound to impress the Board. They are watching me like a hawk anyway.' With these words, Sales Director David Jennings attempts to motivate his staff. And he goes on, 'Surely you must be interested in getting the Board members to notice you. So, do some overtime in the next few months, and stop talking so much about having too much to do and being overworked. One more customer call per day, that is all that is needed. And forget the word "stress" for a change. I count on you! On each and every one of you!' David Jennings is trying to persuade his staff to make an increased effort in the coming year.

He cannot succeed. Why not? Where is he going wrong?

_____

_____

_____

3 Bernard Limming, head of production at a TV station, is asked by the Chief Executive to persuade the staff in the Production Department to accept the new plans for extended working hours. Anticipating the anger of his staff, Bernard Limming aims to show understanding of their feelings and also influence them to accept the changes positively. Full of energy, he starts his explanations, 'We all have to rationalize and pull together to save costs. I am sure we can all put in more effort. Let's put the CEO's suggestions into practice. After all it is not all bad news: we will get paid more, if we succeed.'

After these vigorous sentences, he remembers that he will have to show some empathy as well and finishes on the following note: 'I know that the new working hours will cause some hardship to many of you. It will mean less leisure time and some of our activities outside of work may have to be curtailed. I don't like the new working hours either, but I'm afraid there is no other way'. After Bernard's speech, the colleagues leave the room totally depressed.

Was this the right way to show empathy and project it?

_____

_____

_____

4 Jonathan Marshall, chairman of a world-renowned company producing raw materials, is being urged by the members of the Board to comment on the partly justified rumours about an expected downturn in business in several sectors at the annual top managers' conference, attended by approximately 150 people. He should also stop speculation about a possible merger with, or even takeover by, a foreign corporation.

He prepares his speech well and gets to the root of the factual reasons for the expected trend, categorically denies all rumours and emphatically shows optimism for the future. His strong, elitist leadership style again impresses his audience. At the end, he appeals to all those present to do everything they can for the company – show a better performance, even beyond the call of duty, manage with budgets that have been cut to the bone, try to fulfil the shareholders' justified demands for a bigger return and show understanding and support for the Board. In between, he refers to the annual report and some significant comments. His final sentence is: 'Thank you for your achievements and for your attention'.

He is quite surprised by the rather subdued and cool reaction to his presentation and tells his closest colleagues of his disappointment with the lack of commitment displayed by those present.

Can you understand his disappointment? Could he expect anything else? Why? Would you have chosen another approach?

_____

_____

_____

_____

_____

MASTERING EMPATHY AND PROJECTION

Communication means achieving understanding and acceptance. It also means understanding people, winning them over and influencing them. To achieve this you need to master two qualities: empathy and projection.

Take a piece of paper and draw xy axes on it. The horizontal axis represents empathy understanding others (0–100), pointing to the right. The vertical axis (0–100) is used to record your projection (impact score), increasing from the bottom up. Make a cross where you see your own ability to use empathy and projection successfully. If you consider your empathy and projection skills to be perfect, put a cross in the top right-hand corner of the grid. Just be honest with yourself.

Communication ability diagram

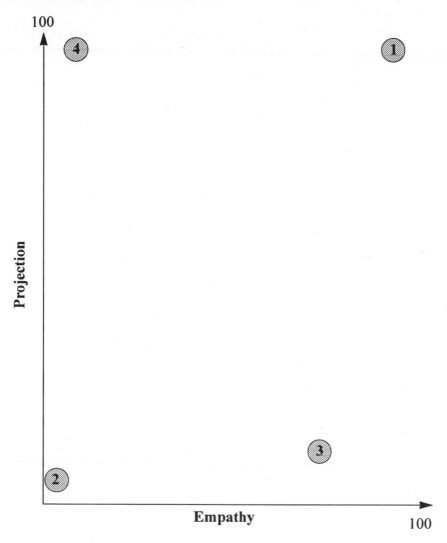

Key:

1 = ideal ability to empathize and project.

2 = minimal ability in both areas.

3 = a lot of empathy, little projection (= a lot of understanding for others, but with little impact on them).

4 = a lot of projection, little empathy (= strong impact, but little understanding for others).

Now analyse the nature and quality of your ability to communicate for the four positions shown in the diagram.

There is hardly anyone who is able to master the two key qualities of communication – empathy and projection – perfectly. The qualities do not occur naturally together either as everyone has different strengths. Some people find it easy to put themselves in someone else's shoes, really feel for them and can always find the right words – comforting, encouraging or motivating. Others can convince others, get their attention, arouse enthusiasm and make them accept and even support their cause. Both empathy and projection are essential for communication, and, don't worry, they can both be developed. On the next few pages, you will see how you can master empathy and projection as a basis for good communication.

Empathy first

Imagine the following situation. You are the owner of a company and have noticed that the sales figures achieved by your sales force in the last quarter are unsatisfactory. You ask your 12 salespeople to come to your office and say, 'You have a tricky job, I am aware of that. Many of our clients are difficult, and are becoming more and more demanding every month. You, as representatives of our company, often have to carry the can for mistakes made in planning, administration, or production.' By using this approach you will be showing empathy for the situation your staff are in. Once you have achieved this, you can use your projection skills, 'But you will have to put in more effort. I'm sure you will all easily manage one additional sales call per day. That will improve your chances of increasing sales by ...'. It is better to use empathy *first* and *then* projection. Your ability to empathize will win your audience and make them receptive for the impact that will follow, 'And we will then all applaud your achievements'.

A vital part of empathy is giving every individual listener the impression that what is being said is meant for the participant personally. This cannot be achieved if you constantly use the word 'I'. The listener will feel that 'you are only talking about yourself, your own interests and feelings'. 'Why does he even pretend he is talking to me?', the listener will say, 'He is only talking to himself'. This damaging self-centredness is one of the main mistakes many speakers make. Count the number of times a speaker says 'I' during a presentation – and do the same for one of your own speeches. Nobody else is interested in 'I', 'me', 'my' or 'for me'. People are really only interested in themselves. So, a speaker who wants to achieve real communication must use 'you' and 'your', or 'we' and 'us'. These are the words needed to win and persuade, because the listeners feel that the speaker is addressing them personally. That often leads to the surprising feeling: he understands me! And that makes the listeners responsive. Everyone has experienced that situation before. Bear it in mind before each speech, even during your planning. Putting the emphasis on 'you' when talking is not an art – it is a question of attitude, self-discipline and practice. This attitude requires a genuine interest in those you are addressing. Given this, the following golden rule will make it easy for you to put it into practice.

You:I = 5:1

In other words, use 'you' five times more often than 'I'. If you take that to heart you will be well received by your participants. The same goes for the wrongly used 'we': the speaker says 'we' but really means 'I'. For example, the businessperson says: 'We want to achieve a higher turnover', but means 'I want ...'. Whenever an 'I' slips out, use 'you' five times. That reduces self-centredness and increases your impact. Self-centredness will not win people, only 'you-centredness' will. Also, 'I' or egocentricity increases stage fright. It separates you from the group. So, for your own sake, use 'you' as much as possible for integration.

The higher a speaker ranks in the company hierarchy, the more difficult it is for him/her to follow the 5:1 rule. Top managers, when addressing their staff almost automatically say, 'I expect all my people to ...', 'I hope that you, John, and you, Margaret, ...', 'I want to show our customers that ...', 'I imagine that ...'. If you train yourself to become 'anti-I', you will actually become allergic to the word. You will notice immediately, when an 'I' escapes you. Turn off your ego-centricity and for every 'I' use 'you' five times to balance your 'empa-thy account'.

Company owners and top executives often have difficulties with empathy, both in their presentation and content. Especially when it is a question of business goals. They assume that their interests and moti-vation and those of the staff are identical. The equation 'what is good for the company is also good for the individual', coupled with the thought that if the individuals do not realize that, they are either stupid or disloyal, is not right. That is why a lot of professional speeches have little effect. Start with the assumption that every employee you address personally feels that their interests are being addressed and can be motivated. But, remember, you have to appeal first and foremost to their No. 1 employer – Me-Myself Ltd.

Also, eliminate all filler words such as 'I think', 'I believe', 'I feel', 'I want' – they only weaken your arguments.

Would you like to learn more about how to express empathy (putting yourself in other people's shoes) in the contents of your presentations? Then you should read the next chapter particularly carefully.

Developing your projection ability

Here are a few helpful tips for developing your projection or impact. Develop your EVA – eyes, voice, attitude – to become charismatic. First, improve your eye contact. Look at all the participants, let your eyes wander and try to attract the eyes of everybody. Stop looking at the ceiling, floor or window. Try to 'hypnotize' people with your eyes. Second, use your voice. A strong voice, clear pronunciation and accen-tuation, simple language and short sentences will create the impression that you are articulate. There is no need for voice and speech training, unless you suffer from noticeable impediments or want to become a professional speaker. Simply taping and videoing yourself will help you develop your skills. Add intensity to create a charismatic persona. This enables you to put your own conviction across. You cannot enthuse and persuade others unless you are enthusiastic yourself and believe in your objective, cause or mission. Third, attitude is liveliness, body language, gestures, drive, dynamism and energy. You cannot make an impact on your participants seated or hidden behind a desk. The closer you are to your group the better. If possible stand face to face. Don't use contrived gestures, but emphasize natural movements and don't stifle them.

In spite of EVA, there is still an ingredient missing. That is your *personality*, your power, your inner strength, your will to persuade. Nothing will go without your suggestive impact, your strong commitment to your cause, your willingness to communicate. If these characteristics are part of the make-up of your personality, so much the better! If not, you can develop them through training, practice and experience. First of all, follow the EVA hints. They will go a long way to helping you. (Look for more tips in the following chapters.)

One last word on the subject of your communication approach: never imitate somebody else. You must be genuine, convincing and yourself. 'Natural'? Yes, but not bland. And do not be content with the way you are. *Everybody* can develop their empathy and projection.

Are you now able to solve the four questions and case studies at the beginning of this chapter?

Make a determined effort to improve both your empathy and projection. They are the two most important qualities of a successful communicator. And always remember the 5:1 rule!

4

REMEMBER EMMA

Can you answer the following four questions?

1 **What does EMMA mean for you in terms of becoming a more effective speaker?**

2 **Does the reason for the participants coming to the event really matter? Aren't the factual contents of the presentation the most important element?**

3 **Why is a careful analysis of what the participants want to hear important, even for an information speech?**

4 **Do you have to bear in mind points such as the general setting of the event, the timing and possible disturbances?**

Can you solve the following four problems?

1 Jeremy Cleary, owner of a rolling mill, makes a mistake almost all bosses make. Can you spot it? At the first meeting of the new year, attended by all members of staff, including his agents, he says, 'We have a problem. Our profit margin has shrunk, and has reached the danger zone. We will have to increase our turnover and reduce our overheads. The structure of our turnover has also changed for the worse – there are too many small orders. And there is too much waste in production. But, I know that you will soon regain control of the situation. After all, we are all in the same boat'.

What do you think goes on in the minds of the employees as they listen to these words, with which their boss wants to harness their commitment to achieving the new year's objectives? Will they do anything to reach that goal?

_____

_____

_____

_____

2 Paul Gregory, Research and Development Manager for an optical instruments company, is over the moon. His department has developed a revolutionary new product. Paul now wants to introduce it to the other members of the staff. He is sure that everyone will be as enthusiastic about the imminent market launch of the product as he is. But he is wrong. The staff react negatively because some of his colleagues do not believe in the success of the new product, the staff of the Marketing Department are despondent because they were involved too late, and a number of people in Production and Administration fear an increase in their workloads.

What are the two main points that Paul has overlooked?

_____

_____

_____

_____

3 A school class visits an important computer software company. It was their maths teacher's idea, as he wants to give his pupils an insight into data processing. He organizes the visit without asking whether or not the pupils are interested. The Managing Director of the company gives a lengthy presentation on the complicated tasks of a software producer. He becomes irritated that after ten minutes a few pupils become restless and disinterested, and seem to be making jokes. After another ten minutes, the teacher interrupts the MD – who is a friend of his – because he realizes that the pupils are not following the presentation at all, and suggests a tour of the company. That arouses interest and the visit ends on a conciliatory note.

What should the teacher and Managing Director have borne in mind?

_____

_____

_____

_____

4 Jodie Fisher has scheduled a meeting for 7 a.m. on Monday. She wants to leave for her holiday in the afternoon and would like, by then, to have finished giving the necessary instructions for the two weeks of her absence. Many of the colleagues she has asked to attend this meeting live a long way from their place of work and have to get up two hours earlier, at 5 a.m. Even her opening sentence, 'Thank you very much for arriving here on time, which I am sure we will all benefit from', causes open displeasure. Everyone knows that Jodie needs her holiday and deserves it, yet the initial negative atmosphere does not improve.

Can a good presentation overcome the consequences of forcing colleagues to attend a meeting against their will?

_____

_____

_____

HOW ENTRENCHED OR FLEXIBLE
ARE ATTITUDES?

Do you know EMMA, an important person in the world of communication? You have to understand her (and respect her) if you want to communicate properly and successfully. The four letters stand for expectations, mentality, motivation and ability of the participants. First of all, try to answer the following questions before you begin to communicate – they are the four crucial factors that affect the reception your participants give your communication.

1 What _expectations_ do the participants bring with them? Positive ones? Negative ones? Neutral? None at all? What do they expect from you? From the occasion? Can you (do you want to) fulfil these expectations? How interested are they? What is the reason for their attendance? Have they come of their own accord? Are they pleased to be there? Is it because of your presentation or for other reasons? Are their expectations conducive to the objective of your communication? What mood are they in?

2 What is their _mentality_? Conservative, progressive? What are their mental characteristics? What is their cultural background? Are they pioneers or followers? Yuppies, workers, entrepreneurs, or specialists?

3 Which _motivations_ of the participants can you appeal to? What do they want? What are their goals? Which of the aspirations of their professional or private lives can you appeal to? How can you inte-

grate those with your own objective? (Please also see the last paragraph in this chapter on this point.)

4 What are they *able* to understand? What is their level of education and knowledge? Are they specialists or laymen? How familiar are they with your topic? Will they understand your jargon? Will they be awake and receptive or too tired to concentrate?

Can you answer these questions? If not, take the trouble to try and find the answers. It is the only way to tailor your presentation to the profile of the participants. And a tailored communication is an absolute prerequisite for successful communication.

If you do not possess all this information, how can you get hold of it? Of course you can argue that all these investigations require a lot of work. This may be true, but:

- you can delegate a large part of them
- correcting the consequences of failed communication will cause you a lot more trouble afterwards than extra work beforehand
- the time required is shorter than you think.

Consider the story of Monsieur Vidal, a French businessman who attended one of our communication seminars, talking on this subject: 'I have to give a technical presentation in Barcelona next Monday. I can answer practically *none* of your questions. Even worse, I don't know whether or not the participants understand French. I am assuming there will be an interpreter, but whether they will interpret simultaneously or consecutively I don't know either. Today is Thursday. This seminar here ends on Saturday. What do you suggest I do?' The friendly, ironical responses on the part of his colleagues 'all you can do is pray', 'close your eyes and go full speed', 'invite the participants to a flamenco evening' – created amusement, but offered no solutions. After lunch, a relieved François Vidal reported back, 'My secretary has just told me that in her view this was the best seminar I'd ever attended. She wants to thank you for your indirect suggestion for her to go to Barcelona immediately to investigate as she's never been there before'. And so it happened. His secretary managed to clarify all the issues on the spot and Vidal told us by fax the following Tuesday that these clarifications had made the difference between an absolute disaster and a complete success.

So, how do you combine EMMA with your objective? On the basis of decades of experience and innumerable speeches made and heard, allow me to give you the following simple tip: write your objective on a small, if possible, standard English business card. Why on an *English* business card? Because they are so small that you can fit on them, at the most, one single objective, one sentence, one or two concepts. There is no room for more! If you try to achieve several objectives with your speech or in a discussion you are likely to achieve none of them. That is why you should make a brief statement of your objective! This applies in particular to information speeches. For example, 'we need new machinery', or 'increase our exports,' or 'generate budget cuts'. Now you need to combine this aim with EMMA – the expectations, mentality, motivation and ability of the participants. This will give you the clue you need – the common objective. And please start with the *participants* not with the *subject*. For example, 'surely you want to ...', 'you must be keen to ...', 'we all have ...', 'we want to achieve together ...'. If you simply cannot find the EMMA clue to which you need to direct your speech, it will remain nothing but a piece of sterile one-way information. Most speakers only think about how they can get their message across. They imagine they can achieve their goal by bombarding the audience with arguments that support their own personal objective. That approach will fail. Only with the opposite can you create true communication: what do the *participants* want? If you start with the expectations, mentality, motivation and attitudes of the participants, you can convey your own message as well. Once more, *first of all*, ask the question: 'What do the participants want?' *Then*, 'Is there a common denominator?' If there is none, there is a one-way flow of information – lecturing, massive pressure, even manipulation = no communication.

> **Look for the common denominator!**

Why *should* your secretary work even more? In order to maintain the company's market share? No. What could persuade a team of employees to work without a pay rise? The fact that the turnover of the company increases again? No. Why should department managers abandon their departmental egoism and strive for better coordination? To enhance the efficient functioning of the company? No. If you as a speaker are aiming for these company objectives – increased workload, no pay rises, close cooperation – you have to recognize the motivations of your target group and use the right appeals to these motives. The common denominator could be, for example, ensuring the survival of the company and, thus, job security. Alternatively, earning twice as much in two years as today. Or less work, less stress, increased productivity, more success. Appealing to these motivations will help you secure your staff's cooperation in achieving your aims.

> **The four questions and case studies should no longer be a problem for you , or are they?**

Communication is rhetoric in reverse. Not getting points across, making plausible, finding the right arguments. Remember also that what is of crucial importance for communication is not what you, the speaker, want, but what the *participants* want! Their expectations, mentality, motivation and ability. You have to make EMMA fully part of your presentation if you are to communicate successfully!

5

TURNING LISTENERS INTO PARTICIPANTS

Can you answer the following four questions?

1 **What is your understanding of two-way communication?**

2 **What is the difference between listeners and participants?**

3 **Have you achieved active participation if your listeners nod in response?**

4 **Does active participation help with stage fright or does it contribute to it?**

Can you solve the following four problems?

1 Dr Arthur Prong describes the export relationship between his country and China in an after-dinner speech at a chamber of commerce. He places the emphasis mainly on economic issues. Dr Prong's speaking style is very good and he delivers his speech fluently. Nevertheless, the listeners remain strangely unmoved. They don't appear to be either involved or concerned. The speech was about an hour long, without breaks, followed by questions. There are very few. There is polite applause at the end. The Chairman thanks Dr Prong for his 'interesting presentation' and hopes that everyone 'learned something of benefit'.

Why was the speech only moderately successful?

_____

_____

_____

_____

2 Eddie Pollard, a dockyard worker, has never had any training in the art of speaking or communication, nor has he ever read anything about rhetoric. Yet he does manage to captivate his colleagues when he talks to them about the future of their jobs and the need to properly organize the new Quality Circles. He is liked by his colleagues, creates an atmosphere of warmth, possesses charisma and invites his listeners again and again to speak their mind, to tell him when they need clarification on a certain point and to correct him if he has misinterpreted their counter-arguments.

What distinguishes Eddie from Dr Prong and other speakers, and what is the reason for his success?

_____

_____

_____

3 The Managing Director of an office equipment manufacturer, Charles Baker, introduces a new social benefit to his staff. He boasts about how he takes the welfare of his employees to heart. That is why, from now on, a fitness instructor will come to the company once a week during working hours and at the company's expense, in order to run fitness and anti-stress courses with the members of staff. Charles also announces a detailed schedule, explaining how to carry out the programme. The reaction to his enthusiastic announcement is one of silence. On leaving the room, one member of staff says to two of his colleagues in a low voice, 'Typical, by order of the boss'. Charles is slightly disappointed. He had expected a positive reaction.

Would it not have been better for Charles to find out beforehand whether or not the suggestion would really be welcomed and so cover himself? He could then have asked for confirmation during his speech, saying, 'As a number of you have told me over the past few weeks, you think this would be a good idea. Is that true? Do most of you share this view? How should we organize this?' This is dialogue, not monologue.

What happens if you, like Charles Baker, do not achieve any Active Participation, for example at a company briefing, even if you are making a good suggestion, one that benefits the workforce rather than the company?

_____

_____

_____

4 Two departmental managers, Tom Jenkins and Jenny Hawthorne, are arguing whether or not 'head-on' lectures should still be used. Tom thinks that they are an outdated form of communication, with no impact, as nowadays no one wants to listen anyway. Jenny counters that the participants could, after all, still be involved. 'And when they make negative comments, how do you deal with those?', Tom wants to know. Jenny argues that negative reactions are better than none at all. If there is no feedback whatsoever, it is like walking on ice that might break at any moment, she adds. 'How about bigger groups of 1 to 200 people though, surely you can't involve every individual?', Tom says. That question leaves Jenny without an answer.

What do you think?

_____

_____

_____

HOW TO GET PEOPLE TO PARTICIPATE

'Those who want to speak must be able to listen' goes the proverb. That is true. But, you say, 'Hardly anyone is willing to listen any more'. To a certain extent that is true as well. Mainly due to the easily consumable mass media and today's acoustic and visual overstimulation, hardly anyone wants to – or is able to – listen with concentration to a speech for a long period of time. Many people nowadays consider that a speech of more than 30 to 40 minutes is an unreasonable demand on them. In other words if you stand in front of the audience and give a two-hour head-on lecture, you cannot get anyone to listen – unless you are an exceptional personality or a gifted star speaker, such as Ronald Reagan or, Winston Churchill. A good communicator knows that and acts accordingly.

Initially, most people facing you are only listeners. Some of them don't listen at all; others _hear_ but don't _listen_. Having to listen passively to a long monologue _is_ a strain – if the speaker does not involve the audience. That is the solution to the riddle. Communication can only be achieved by means of a two-way process, an exchange of thoughts. There is no such thing as one-way communication – the definition of communication makes that concept absurd. The sender is at the same time a receiver and vice versa. There always has to be a distinct interaction between speaker and listener. If that is not taken into consideration – and there are some speakers with good rhetorical and stylistic skills who do not realize this – you cannot communicate.

Monologues will not captivate an audience and will never free the speaker from mental isolation.

This is why the core point of our communication training method, which has been experienced and tested the world over, is *two-way* communication. It means establishing a dialogue, which, in turn, means turning your listeners into participants. How? There is a whole series of techniques available. The most important one is active participation (AP). Here are 12 examples. You can activate your participants by, for instance:

 1 directly involving the people you are talking to
 2 asking the participants questions
 3 calling for agreement
 4 inviting voicing of opinions
 5 making them do something (give them tasks)
 6 soliciting examples
 7 letting them fill in gaps
 8 making them ask questions
 9 (constantly) stimulating discussions among them
10 checking their understanding
11 asking them to contribute (examples)
12 inviting them to quote their experiences.

Active participation – involving the participants – creates dialogue and feedback. A speaker who achieves AP creates true communication. Nothing more is needed to make you a true communicator.

> **Turn listeners into participants. That's the way to win people. Participants are contributors, supporters, partners, allies.**

As the speaker, you can only *instigate* AP. Only when there is a reaction, however – in the form of a contribution in return or an answer from a participant – have you *achieved* AP. Imagine, for example, that you are asking a question and don't get an answer. That can mean a lot or nothing at all. First of all, it is, at best, simply a reaction. It is passive participation (PP). Thus, it is not yet a dialogue. In the same way that a pure nodding of the head may mean nothing at all – sometimes it just precedes someone nodding off – or it may be just an automatic reflex reaction to the boss. Passive participation is not enough. Participation has to be active, noticeable and, furthermore, positive.

'Do you agree with me?' If the answer you get to this is 'No', then you have negative active participation (NAP). Anything that gives the participants the feeling of no longer being a listener, but a 'contributor', even answering 'No', creates participation. Here are some examples. You can easily find more. 'Are you with me?', 'Is this explanation sufficient?', 'Would you look at it in this way, too?', 'Have we covered this area sufficiently?', 'Would you like some more examples to illustrate this point?', 'Any ideas about this?', 'Do you accept this analysis?', 'What do you think?', 'Could you think of an example here?', 'Is there anything else you'd like to know about this?', 'What do you say to this?', 'Doesn't that make you wonder whether ...?', 'What is your reaction to this?', 'Could you make a note of this?', 'What do you think is missing here?', 'Could I ask you to ...', 'How does that feel from your point of view?', 'Is this acceptable?'

Distinguish between 'closed' questions – that can only be answered with a 'Yes' or 'No' ('Do you agree?') – and 'open' questions – which cannot be answered with just 'Yes' or 'No' and, thus, require a more extensive response 'What is your view on this?'. A closed question is also a control question, used to check understanding or to obtain agreement from your participants, such as, 'Is that correct?', 'Shall I continue?', 'Is this too fast?' A yes or no response, however, does not tell you much. If you want to achieve a *real* dialogue and exchange of thoughts, use more open questions, such as, 'What is your opinion on this?', 'How would you do it?'

When should you start AP? *Right at the beginning!* It establishes contact, creates confidence and common ground, as well as setting the scene for what follows. Make this initial participation as easy as possible for your audience. Ask leading questions, such as, 'Is that OK like this?', 'Can we proceed like this?', 'Are you truly interested in working together in the best possible way?' This will get the communication going. But, insist on a reply, otherwise you will get PP – and you risk another PP when you ask your next question. If, during your speech, you want to emphasize a certain point and elucidate it further, you could, for example, ask the participants, 'What is your understanding of this?' This not only allows you to see whether or not your thought has been understood, it also means that you have established a relationship with the participants that you can use to obtain further information and increase understanding. Even an AP that has been solicited before the start is an effective opening: 'You told me before this meeting that this subject is of particular interest to you, could you briefly tell me again why?'

In *information* speeches, you should use a lot of control questions – after all, you want to know whether (or how) the participants have understood your statements. This is not essential when giving an *occasion* speech, as its aim is mainly to involve the participants on an emotional level, to create a feeling of belonging and mutual liking. In *motivation* speeches, success depends on AP creating enthusiasm: 'Do we really want to win this game against our arch rivals?', the trainer asks his team. The team's response must be a strong 'yes', otherwise you can forget about winning the game altogether. In *persuasion* speeches AP has to underline common ground, whereas in *action* speeches you use it to achieve a binding decision (see Chapters 10, 11 and 12 for more).

There are only three instances where AP is often *inappropriate*. A speech at a funeral, a disciplinary speech, where one-way expression *is* intended, and when there is a strong conflict as this does not allow for real communication. These are the only three exceptions.

Here are some more examples of how to actively involve the participants. You can, for instance, build in questions during your speech ('Would you have thought that?' 'Do you agree?'). A good example is the following: During a staff meeting, the Chief Executive of the German subsidiary of a large American firm wants to praise a colleague who, on his own, had been responsible for the entire advertising activity of the company. He has the following idea for AP. He asks people from one department after another to stand up and applaud themselves. First, the members of Production, then Sales, followed by Purchasing and Accounts. Finally, he asks Advertising to stand up.

When the only member of that 'one-man team' gets up to clap his hands, the Chief Executive says, 'You have more than deserved your applause'. What happens? The whole amazed assembly stands up and applauds their colleague. Hardly anyone knew until then that he is the sole person in charge of all advertising.

The following example proves that it is possible to achieve AP even in church, at a wedding. A young couple get married in the presence of their friends in a small church. A few weeks before the wedding, the clergyman who is to marry the couple asks the witnesses to prepare a little speech of five minutes each. During the ceremony, they both express their personal best wishes to the couple in front of the altar. Before giving the wedding rings to the couple to exchange, the parson asks the guests to pass them round and says, 'Please hold both rings in your hands for a few seconds and then express your thoughts and wishes to our couple'. They all do – it is a memorable experience, not only for the couple, but also for all the guests at the ceremony.

At an international management conference, the speaker asks the participants to express what they think are the three most important leadership qualities. The statements are all collected, compiled, handed out to the participants during a break and then discussed in the whole group – and that with 300 participants. Our communication training seminars – where all the methods recommended here are tested and practised – are not opened by the trainer, but by one of the participants. Then, everyone speaks for one minute in front of a video camera on the subject 'What is communication?' And everyone explains what they hope to gain from the seminar.

During an enlarged Board meeting held to decide on the advertising budget, the attendees are asked to decide between a maximum and a minimum solution, and also evaluate the effectiveness of each of five advertising slogans.

At a fiftieth birthday party, each of the guests is invited to tell a short anecdote about their contact with the person to be honoured. Does it work? And how! The only problem is that everyone wants to say something, which takes time – 50 minutes in this instance, to be precise. But no one noticed and no one minded. Can you imagine a 50-minute monologue at a birthday party?

During a sales conference, the participants are asked to look under the seat of their chairs. There they find a piece of paper on which is a competition on the qualities of a new product. The first ten correct answers win instant prizes.

These few examples illustrate the variety and diversity of methods available to achieve AP. *Positive active participation* is a priceless communication tool. No matter how brilliantly you formulate your sentences in a monologue, they cannot replace active participation.

And do you know about the most useful added bonus that AP can have for you? If you manage to establish real contact with the participants through AP from the beginning, you will notice that you will lose most of your stage fright. Dialogue breaks down tension and stress. The feedback you get from the participants gives you reassurance, which, in turn, has a calming effect on your pulse rate. Besides, it shows that you are in control!

Of course, you need to practise AP. You should use the broad spectrum of AP methods available to you in communication whenever the occasion arises, to avoid them getting rusty and contrived. You can train in the use of AP with friends or colleagues, then use it for real in every conversation, every negotiation, every meeting. In spite of this, there remains a certain risk in complicated real-life situations. Yet, there is a way to avoid that too. A Board member who wanted to use a certain AP during a shareholders' meeting and had practised it beforehand with his colleagues, nearly came unstuck with it on the day. At the beginning of his presentation he addressed the shareholders with the statement, 'Would those of you who are against achieving growth in our business please stand up.' To his surprise, several dozen shareholders did stand up – members of an alternative movement. They had become shareholders in order to undermine the company's business policies. During the rehearsal with his colleagues, no one had stood up – not even as a warning. Everyone was in favour of expansion. Not all the shareholders were, though. Consequently, it is important to analyse the motives of *all* the participants and formulate the APs accordingly. If he had said, 'Whoever is against reasonable, controlled growth, which would safeguard our jobs and earn you a nice profit on top please stand up?', he would have been successful. The Chairman of the Board cleverly extricated himself from this embarrassing situation by using a *second* AP – *asking* the silent majority to stand up as well.

> **Go back to the beginning of the chapter: I am sure you are now able to solve the four questions and case studies**

You turn listeners into participants through AP. Involving the participants creates feedback which gives you confidence. Only two-way communication is communication. Thus, no more monologues, but, rather, dialogues. That's the golden rule for your success.

6

FINDING A CAPTIVATING START

Can you answer the following four questions?

1 Do you have to welcome everyone present at the beginning of
your speech?

2 Can you start a speech with the end?

3 Do you know when you can start a speech with a joke and when
you cannot?

4 Is it possible for someone else to start off your speech?

Can you solve the following four problems?

1 'Ladies and gentlemen. Unprepared as I unfortunately am due to circumstances beyond my control and possessing a lot less expert knowledge on the subject than most of you, I will, nevertheless, try to give
you a comprehensive overview of the various organizational cost analysis methods and – if you will allow me – I would like to start by briefly
mentioning the historical background conditions, which I am sure you,
for the most part, will already know, but nevertheless ...'

Stop!

Dr Messer, Ph.D. in business economics and Finance Director of a
large soft drinks company, has been asked by the employers' association to talk about his company's experience of using various cost
analysis methods. As Dr Messer is very honoured by this request, but
is afraid of making a fool of himself, he has read up on the subject very
carefully to refresh his memory. Then he wrote down his speech.
Unfortunately, he did not have enough time to rehearse it. Dr Messer
was sure that once he 'got into' the subject he would be able to give a
decent presentation.

Why does Dr Messer come across as obsequious rather than self-confident? What do you think was his intention in starting his speech like this?

---

2 Anthony Campbell, an architect, has been asked to give a presentation to the local architects' association on council regulations governing the conversion of multistorey buildings. He knows that his colleagues and listeners are dreading the lecture, which is scheduled to take two hours. They will be drowned in legal rules and regulations, interpretations and guidelines. Anthony wonders how he can make this information, which is dry yet important for their daily work – more interesting and, above all, how he can find an opening so exciting that it will arouse his participants' curiosity.

He structures the subject into three main areas and then writes down the following sentence as his first one, 'In principle, there are only three things you have to remember. If you manage those, the rest is only a question of consulting the relevant literature and that can be done by someone other than yourself. First of all, it is essential to ...'.

What do you think of this opening?

---

3 Two heads of department are preparing their six-monthly report for the Board meeting. They have a discussion about how they should start their presentations. 'Well, I am going to start in the same way as last time: factual, logical information, which should be comprehensible for anyone. The facts, figures and trends are all in the handout, so people can follow them while I talk.' His colleague argues that, after all, the members of the Board are only human like everyone else, and want to have a laugh and be entertained now and then: 'I'm first going to tell the story of the customer who thought chips were a potato product and asked me what they'd got to do with computer processors! That is quite amusing, but also has a point. We are still far too technical in our advertising'.

Would you start a report to your bosses in this way? And if you were the chief executive wouldn't you ask the second speaker to come to the point?

_____

_____

_____

_____

_____

4 John Lucas has been invited to talk at a debate, along with four other speakers. The organizer of the event has allocated every speaker five minutes to present their respective points of view. John thinks that this is far too short and he tells his audience so immediately: 'Good evening, ladies and gentlemen, lord mayor, senator, minister, members of the press, distinguished guests. I am particularly delighted to have the opportunity to speak to you tonight. The five minutes I have been given are unfortunately not long enough to ... It is thus not possible ...'.

John Lucas has made almost all the mistakes that can possibly be made in so few words. Can you find a better, more exciting, opening?

HOW DO YOU START REALLY WELL?

The first sentence of a speech is the second most important one. Which one is more important still? Yes, the last sentence. The beginning and the end – the promising start and the desirable goal to be achieved – are the decisive stages in every speech. A successful beginning; for example, an AP with the audience establishes contact, arouses curiosity and gives you self-confidence. This is good for the participants, because they feel involved, and good for you, because it helps you over the most difficult stage in every speech – the beginning. It also helps you to get rid of your stage fright.

Take great care to find a captivating opening. It is your first stepping stone towards success. Your first sentence lays the foundation. But how do you start a speech? Under no circumstances should you start with the following:

1 apologies
2 long introductions
3 warming (or tuning) up
4 fishing for compliments
5 self-centred reflections
6 justifications for talking
7 subservience
8 'Good morning' (at 11.30 a.m.)

9 negative beginnings ('I will not today ...') or false promises ('I will try and be brief')

10 the stereotyped 'ladies and gentlemen' (or directly addressing certain distinguished attendees) as you can put your welcome into your second sentence.

None of these will help you get off to a flying start. Here is an opening that guarantees success. Begin with an IBP. This stands for initial benefit promise. In other words, how will *you*, the participants, benefit from listening to me? Example, 'In the next four minutes, you will learn four new ways of achieving more by doing less'. This is an example of how you promise a benefit of listening to you. Yet, this is only one possibility; there are numerous others. You will get to know them. But, how do you find the best opening? Having compiled your speech guide (list of key words) and written it down in even fewer key words and having found an effective ending, a tip is to pick five to eight possible options from the list of good speech openings. Check whether these can be left out without a loss of impact. If they can, cross them out. Then, choose the best one from among those that are left.

> **Find an exciting, captivating, promising opening and you have won half the battle.**

Allow yourself enough time to find an effective opening, too. Successful communicators often ponder for *hours* over the first three sentences of their speech. They know that the beginning of their speech sets the course for success or failure: a good start points towards plain sailing, a bad one makes you sail constantly against the wind.

Below you will find a selection of successful openings – 24 tested speech openings that create excitement, curiosity, contact, positive feelings and impact.

1 The subject itself

If the subject is attractive, jump straight into it! No welcoming remarks, no long-winded introductions, get straight to the point instead and arouse interest! The participants will show their gratitude by paying attention and will assume that you'll continue your speech in the same way, concentrating on essentials. Quote the subject in your first sentence ('Reducing costs while avoiding harmful side-effects, that is the issue') or only the key word ('Innovation – certainly, but how?') A short headline is another possibility: '(the year), a year full of problems, prospects, real opportunities'. By the way, take great care to choose the right words to introduce your subject. 'Basic considerations about measures to improve exports', will certainly arouse less enthusiasm than 'Can short-term measures to improve exports really help us?' A few additional tips: a good opening resembles the caption of an advertisement. Take a look at a few and at some newspaper head-lines. Don't use more than eight words and begin with a question that arouses curiosity or contains a benefit – or even a solution. For example, 'How to improve creativity in our company'. And if you, as the speaker, are presented with a subject expressed with a poor choice of words, react with suggestions as to how to improve it.

2 Highlight the contents to arouse interest

A brief hint at the contents of your speech can arouse interest. How do you do that? Like this, for example: '9 November 1989 – a date we will never forget. Do you still remember what happened?' This will evoke memories. Or a speaker may ask about it in the first sentence. For instance, 'Low oil prices – good or bad for industry, for the environment?' This is a question most of the participants will probably be familiar with. As the speaker does not give any clue about their own opinion at the start, participants will be curious about what is going to follow. Such an opening can be used for almost any subject. A spectacles manufacturer began a presentation to department stores' buyers with, 'Did you know that more than one in four people are short-sighted?'

3 Rhetorical questions, genuine, short questions and factual questions

Using a question at the beginning of your speech helps you achieve several benefits at the same time: you establish contact with the participants, arouse interest investigate the atmosphere and the expectations of the participants, and you reduce your own tension. Furthermore, it gives you breathing space as it invites answers from the participants. You can ask up to three questions here. If you want to start with rhetorical questions, apply the rule of three. 'Who really cares if young people don't see a future for their jobs any more? Does this not affect all of us in one way or another? Should we not spend a couple of minutes on this subject?'

Genuine, short questions – whether closed or open, alternative or single-issue – can always be found. Here is an example of an alternative question: 'The choice is obvious: to expand or close down?' If you want to avoid provoking long-winded answers or discussions in reply to a factual question, you should formulate it as a closed – yes/no – question: 'Stopping low-altitude flights. Is that the right decision? What do you think?' The answer to this can be 'Yes' or 'No'. 'Do you know how many credit cards the average person owns nowadays?' This genuine, short question was the hook used by a banker to introduce the subject of personal credit.

4 Original comments highlighting the occasion

'Can you remember what happened 15 billion years ago? The Big Bang. Do you know what happened four million years ago? The formation of the Earth. And one or two million years ago? The first human beings began to develop. Five hundred years ago? The Middle Ages. Now imagine the past 15 billion years as a single year: On 1 January there was the Big Bang, the Earth began to form in September, the human race on 31 December and the Middle Ages took place one hour before midnight.' This is how a presentation about the development of the Federal Republic of Germany after the Second World War started.

A good opening will win you the support of the participants and arouse interest, as you are signalling that the rest of your speech will be just as exciting and entertaining. But you don't always have to dive so deep into history: 'Exactly ten years ago today, three men were sitting in this room ...' or 'What special day is today?' Pause. This provides different answers from the participants, after which the speaker resumes: 'For the first time in the history of our company, we have achieved a daily output of ....That is a record for our industry!'

5 Addressing the audience directly – appealing to their motivation

'More than 2000 years of engineering experience are sitting in this room. Each one of you, 200 altogether, has on average 10 years' experience, if not more. If you add mine, that makes 2020.' Such an opening – and this again is another tested example – breaks the ice between speaker and participants, gets the participants to think in a positive way and makes them feel good and proud. Here is another unusual, motivating start: 'Thank you very much for what you have done and congratulations. You are a super team. Without you in production we would never have achieved this.'

6 Shock statement

No one expects that when the company boss gets up at the briefing he will say bluntly, 'It is 5 minutes to 12 on our clock of destiny. We really are in a sad state. If we don't immediately ...' He follows this with a dramatic description of the company's situation, which shakes up the members of his staff. Using this as his introductory statement, the boss impresses his colleagues and thus makes them receptive. The Board meeting preceding this briefing had started like this: 'Yes, next year will be crucial. If we go on like this we will be making a loss of 50 million pounds in two years' time.' 'It has happened. We did not expect this. It is tough news', is another example. Sometimes you have to shake people up to create a response.

7 Jokes, anecdotes, quotes, episodes, stories, examples

If you, as the speaker, want to say something funny, then go ahead – it is quite unusual. It can turn around a morose atmosphere completely. But, be careful – choose the right jokes, anecdotes, etc., and remember them well. An inappropriate joke or one that is misunderstood by some of the participants or an anecdote with a messed-up punchline will cause embarrassment. Try out these openings beforehand. Jokes have the best effect when they are unexpected, so never announce them: 'To start with a nice little story ...'. Nor this one either: 'A really true story, you may not believe it, but ...' Many will start doubting it then. Don't laugh beforehand. Don't say after the joke or anecdote, 'And now back to our subject'. Check quotations carefully. Always use the present tense. Don't narrate an event strictly chronologically. Avoid using ego-centric episodes – (unless it was you who got caught out). When in doubt, use KISS: keep it short and simple. It is safer that way. If no one laughs, don't explain a punchline . You might still have been under-stood despite an occasional barrier to laughter. There are audiences that don't like to laugh, even though they are amused.

8 A memorable common experience

You can create common ground for communication by recalling a common experience at the beginning of your speech that everyone likes to remember: '1988, the Conference Centre in the Cotswolds. Do you remember how ...' Or, 'How wrong we all were in our estimates then. Ten per cent higher sales was the daring prediction. Do you remember?' People will nod. Your enthusiasm will spread among the participants; communication is achieved. Now you can get your thoughts across.

9 Audio-visual effects

An exciting opening can also be created by performing a sketch, played by members of your staff or colleagues (a customer calling to com-plain, for example); or a slide that gets the participants in the mood, a caricature or illustration projected on the wall; an object (such as your product); a demonstration, a video or any other audio-visual aid that will arouse people's interest. However, the acoustic or visual effect used has to be easy to understand, read or see for the participants. Do you remember Ghandi's handful of rice, Khrushchev's shoe during his speech at the UN, Hamlet with the skull?

10 Personal confession

Admitting a mistake, a gap in one's knowledge or an inability to do something undoubtedly makes for an exciting opening as well. As personal confessions are unusual, they have a special positive effect. So, why not admit a possible weakness, provided you have enough self-confidence? 'I made a real mistake when I dismissed Paul Brown.' Such a confession can be coupled with an appeal to the participants: 'Without you we will not be able to get out of this'. Another example: 'Hopefully *you* can find the answer – I haven't been able to so far.'

11 Current events or news items

A speaker who takes up a current event, news item or a piece of interesting information at the beginning of a speech comes across as flexible and unconventional. And you create strong curiosity. The most effective items are things that may have happened in the meeting room, the conference hotel or the company: 'At the entrance, our most senior colleague told me ...'. A politician once did the following: 'I have carefully followed the statements of the previous speaker and have written down all his convincing arguments on this sheet of paper' and he then held up a white, blank sheet of paper. Not entirely fair, maybe, but effective. Current news items taken from radio, TV or newspapers can be used equally well to start off a speech: 'In today's *Financial Times* you can read the following on the front page', 'On the news this morning ...'. You could also read out a fax or quote figures that none of the participants knows about yet.

12 'Imagine ...'

'... our cash flow has gone down by another five per cent in the last quarter.' How's that for a start with a bang? It invites the participants to get involved, to visualize something. 'Imagine you have grown up on a desert island and are confronted with a personal computer for the first time in your life.' This creates an image in the minds of the participants that you can go back to and use again during the course of your speech: 'How would you use this PC to ...?' Just start with the word 'Imagine'.

13 Analogies

Speakers frequently use analogies or comparisons. If they are accurate, they will impress, but if they are used in the wrong context, they can become dangerous. 'Top executives are like racehorses – able to perform but are also sensitive.' Sounds positive, but not to older managers. 'Leading staff is like raising kids.' You could say that in front of personnel managers, but not in front of union representatives, when it would be dangerous. No problems are caused by analogies such as 'Passion in politics may be a good motor, but a bad steering wheel.'

14 Contrasting ideas – using antithesis

'The decision you are facing is like the one of deciding between armament and disarmament, defeat and victory, or bankruptcy and expansion.' When using antithesis, it is preferable to mention the negative statement first, then the positive one. This allows you to come back to it immediately in your second sentence: 'Disarmament is obviously our aim, yet ...', or, 'Victory is what we are after, as ...', or, 'Expansion is the only right decision, because ...'. You all know the antithetical phrase from Hamlet. Adapt it to your own purposes: 'To be or not to be successful in this most competitive market is the challenge we are facing today'. But, be careful not to become overdramatic!

15 Off-beat, unconventional and unusual openings

'Would you please take a piece of paper and write down one word –
only one – that comes to mind when you think about today's subject of
"company conflict".' Pause. 'Who has written something that is similar
to "serious" or "find solution"? Please raise your hands. Result? Over
80 per cent! All right, let's search, as the situation is serious indeed.'
Better than a lengthy introduction to the subject, isn't it? Or, 'You've
come to this meeting expecting that ..., but you will experience the
opposite.' Such a beginning literally provokes the audience into paying
attention, which is exactly what you want to achieve. One last example:
'You want a quick decision. But the more we push, the slower we will
progress.'

16 Start a dialogue with participants or colleagues, get
someone else to open

Why do you have to find the first words? Let someone else begin or two
of you do it together! 'John, you are our most experienced engineer,
what do you think?' You could also begin by asking for a show of
hands: 'How many of you are definitely in favour of cleaner air in the
office?' As you can be pretty sure in advance that an overwhelming
majority *will* be in favour, you can use the vote as the basis for your
next few sentences. You want to talk about new safety measures at
work and have heard that Tim Brown recently stumbled over a brick
that had fallen off the top of a wall: 'Tim, could you tell us what happened to you yesterday'. Starting a dialogue with the participants right
at the outset of your presentation lets you establish contact and thus
communication. It relieves you of stress and reduces stagefright.

17 Activate the participants, by introducing them to each other

Such an opening can have an electrifying, positive effect on the whole
atmosphere in the room. 'Have you said "Hello" to your neighbour yet?
Why don't you tell each other why you are here today'. You have acti-
vated the participants, established contact among them, loosened up
the atmosphere and created a group climate that will lead instantly to

real communication. Another example: 'Write down the first word that comes to your mind when you think about the subject X. Now compare what you have written with your neighbours'. Here, too, you are shifting the focus of activity – the *participants* have to do something, you will win time, you can take a breather and reduce your stage fright.

Does it work? Of course! Always? Yes, always! People *want* to talk to each other.

18 'Only three points ...'

Day in, day out we all have to listen to discussions, speeches, thoughts and statements from others and are grateful to any speaker who tells us, even in the first few sentences, that their presentation will contain no more than three important points. Tell people right at the start: 'There are only three things to bear in mind when playing golf ...'. Three is a magic figure. Every participant is able to remember three points. The boss says to his heads of department, 'There are only three things that count: performance, profit and the future'. Delight your listeners with an easy concept: 'Innovation consists of only three parts: defining the problem, searching for ideas and practical implementation. Everything else is less important'. Do you find this too simple? Consciously simplifying complicated processes and concepts will get you further than complicated descriptions of simple things.

19 'You'/ 'We', primary motives

Striving for prestige, monetary rewards, love, security, curiosity, comfort, support and health – the list of motivating factors is long. Referring to primary motives has a very special effect on people. They get underneath people's skin. Here are four examples: 'Success is ours. We only need to grab it.', 'It's a great feeling having accomplished a true achievement, isn't it?', 'Hitting the competition on the head is fun, isn't it?' and 'You are looking for a purpose to your commitment. So are we. You want to safeguard the future. So do we.'

20 Begin with the conclusion

Think about the novels or films that start with the end. Such an opening creates suspense for the readers or viewers, as they now want to know how this end came about. You, too, can use this technique. State your conclusion at the beginning: 'Yes, we can fulfil your expectations completely', begins the speaker at a discussion, and in the minutes that follow the conditions under which these expectations can be fulfilled are explained. A design and development director wants to motivate his designers and begins his talk by saying: 'We can do it again this time. And this is how: ...'. Why don't you try this approach?

21 Start among the participants

Entertainers sometimes start their shows in this way. They don't stand on the stage. Instead, they are in the auditorium, among the audience. You can do that, too. Instead of going to the front before your speech, start talking from among the group of participants. This will come as a complete surprise to the shareholders at an annual general meeting, for example, or the members of staff at a company briefing and will work to your advantage. You will achieve friendly attention. Beginning your speech from among the plenary group shows solidarity with the participants – one of us, from among us – and it is original. But, prepare such a beginning carefully. Where will you sit? How can you go to the front? Can the technological support cope with this? Maybe you need a different microphone for your spectacular entrance, or stairs to the platform. Practise it!

22 Loud, slow, emphatic

It is not only *what* you say that is important for a good, exciting opening, but also *how* you say it. The participants must be able to tell from the mere tone of your voice that your presentation is important. That is why you have to clearly emphasize the beginning – speak loudly, slowly and emphatically! It is important to realize the significance of this simple advice. Especially at the beginning, speakers often talk too low, too fast and too softly.

23 The IBP: immediately promise a benefit to your listeners

Any start is difficult, for you and also for the participants. Thus, give them a positive, tempting message at the beginning as a reward for their attendance. 'After only five minutes, you will realize how ...'. The promise of a benefit at the start motivates the participants to listen and take in your message. 'The first three suggestions will instantly show you that ...'. By creating a loop that links an exciting opening with a powerful finish, you can extend the promise of a benefit given in the first few sentences right through to the end: 'At the end of this present-ation you will have received at least ten good tips also for how you can really motivate your staff'. This extends the participants' span of atten-tion.

24 Other openings

Use ideas of your own. There are so many possibilities – new and unconventional ones, too. Look for a method that fits your personality. 'Those who go where no one else has gone before leave their mark and not only dust.' A wise saying, isn't it?

One more thing: why do most speakers begin with 'Ladies and gen-tlemen'? Probably because they don't know how to begin in any other way. You do now and you can insert the 'ladies and gentlemen' open-ing, if need be, in your second or third sentence. It would at least be observed.

So, test your opening. If you can leave it out and it's not a loss, look for a better one! And then, practise! If your first sentence does not make an impact, you will lose your chance for immediate success. You only have one chance to make a good first impression.

> Can you now answer the four questions and solve
> the four problems at the beginning of this chapter?

This has been a fairly long chapter. From this fact alone you can see how important a successful opening is. During our communication seminars, we spend hours working out good openings and practising them. An exciting opening is more important than a good main part. You have to win your participants instantly. Learn the first few sentences of your speech by heart, so they really work.

7

CHOOSING A COMPELLING CLOSE

Can you answer the following four questions?

1 **What is better for the speaker: if the participants interrupt with their questions or if questions are asked at the end of the speech?**

2 **Can you salvage a mediocre speech with a brilliant close?**

3 **Which ending is better: 'Good luck' or 'Thank you very much' or are both of them bad?**

4 **Should you announce the end of your speech in advance?**

Can you solve the following four problems?

1 Mike Wilson and Chris Tanner are production managers in a car factory. They want to give a presentation on the issue of safety at work to the trainees in their areas. Mike argues that they should not only point out the dangers inherent in factory work to the young people, but also outline the benefits to them of abiding by the safety regulations. He intends to finish with the words 'Safety at work – that means for you: health, secure careers, status.'

Chris, on the other hand, would prefer to impress the trainees, shake them, tell them about accidents at work and their frightening consequences. At the end she wants to appeal to the young people: 'We hope that something like this will never happen here!'

Both managers have good intentions. But only one of them has found a good conclusion? Which one? And why?

_____

_____

_____

2 During his speech at a chamber of commerce, which was scheduled to last 40 minutes, Victor Ross realizes that he is going to finish much earlier than planned. The reason? He had expected a lot more questions. What now? There are three possibilities: he could either drag out the subject a bit; or he could finish his speech as planned, but 15 minutes earlier; or he could surprise the participants by saying, 'And now, 15 minutes earlier than planned, we can finish. But let me just briefly sum up the most important points again. Is that OK? Right!'

Which solution would you advise Victor to take?

_____

_____

_____

3 The Personnel Director of a large pharmaceutical company is giving a presentation to his senior managers on the interim results of staff reduction measures that had been decided on a year ago by the Board. He prepares his speech very well. He praises the senior managers for their help in implementing the measures and, after his final words, he even gets applause. The next day, the Personnel Director talks in front of the company's union representatives. He thanks them, too, for their understanding and asks them not to obstruct the measures of the Board in the future either. As his closing words were such a success with the senior managers, he uses them again here, '... if we continue like this, we will make it'. Not a single hand moves. The Personnel Director creeps back to his seat like a beaten dog and thinks, 'Typical! Union people don't have the slightest understanding of the measures necessary to save the company'.

He is wrong. It is entirely his fault. He could easily have had a positive response, if he had ... well, what should he have done differently?

_____

_____

_____

_____

4 'I want the participants to feel that I am extemporizing. I will not learn a single sentence by heart, but will follow my intuition – even with the beginning and the end – and play it according to the climate of the meeting.'

What do you think of this approach? Would you recommend a speaker to rely solely on intuition and experience and to tailor both the opening and the closing of the speech according to the mood of the participants?

_____

_____

_____

_____

THE CRUCIAL CLOSE

The most important part of a speech is the end. No other part in the entire presentation is as crucial to its success as the last. A bad ending can ruin even the best speech. A good ending, however, can salvage even a mediocre speech. How come? The answer is simple: the ending is the last, remaining impression in the minds of the participants. After your last sentence the participants must feel compelled to think, 'That was really good', or, 'I will remember this'. What applies to an appropriate, exciting opening also applies to a gripping close. Consider some of the 15 different possibilities listed on the following pages.

> **Test their impact and then choose the conclusion you think is best for your speech. When practising, leave out the last few sentences as an experiment. Did you lose anything?**

Is your speech still the same, or have you inadvertently packed some additional ideas into the last few sentences? If yes, cut them out!

> **Do not introduce new ideas in your conclusion – otherwise you will not have any conclusion.**

Mistakes made time and time again

1 Speakers frequently finish by saying, 'Thank you very much'. That really is the most unimaginative ending. Thank you for what? Who has been doing the hard work here? If, unfortunately, it was the audience, even your 'thank you' won't help you. There are variations of this bad habit, such as, 'Thank you very much for your attention', or, 'I thank you', or, 'Many thanks for listening'. Skip it! No good speaker has to

thank the participants for anything at the end of a presentation. So why do so many do it?

- Because they have copied it from others without thinking about it.

- Because they cannot think of anything to say once they are through with their subject matter.

- Because they believe this will earn them the participants' gratitude.

- Because they cannot find a proper ending.

'That's it!' is another ending without ending. Or: 'This is all I wanted to say on the subject'.

2 Fishing for compliments is very widespread, too – and very dangerous as a conclusion. 'I would be happy if my speech has given you some new ideas or increased your understanding of the subject?', or, 'I hope that my presentation was not completely uninteresting for you'. These are clumsy attempts to try and coax the participants into a positive reaction. Their reaction can also be negative, however. A dead silence will show their disapproval. This is not only true for the conclusion of a speech. Fishing for compliments should be banned from all parts of a presentation. It places the wrong emphasis – and creates a bad impression. Test your own reactions as a participant when a speaker woos recognition, compliments and applause.

3 You should also forget the word 'I' when planning a good conclusion to your speech. After all, the event is not about you, but about the participants.

4 It is dangerous to invite the participants to ask questions at the end of a presentation. Don't let yourself be tempted into it just because it is done so frequently. Mistakes made by others should not be your yardstick. The potentially good effect of a speech is endangered when your last word is possibly followed by criticism that confuses you or weakens your final point; if you are bombarded with questions; if an argument breaks out; or if there are no questions at all. It is even more embarrassing, when that's the end as you will then hardly have the opportunity to 'straighten things out'. Discussions almost automatically divide people, rather than bring them together. It is far better to invite the participants right at the start to ask their questions instantly and throughout the speech whenever they arise! That is real communication! You will get feedback (AP), a feeling for the audience and their attitudes. And the audience will appreciate that. All this livens up the atmosphere and no one can blame you for not letting the participants have a say. And, finally, you can orchestrate your own conclusion by choosing your own compelling or meaningful last few sentences.

5 Repeatedly announcing the end, which then still does not come, strains the nerves of the participants, who, torn between hope and disappointment, may even become openly aggressive. Should a conclusion be announced at all? If you want to make sure that the participants will take it in, yes. But then come to the end quickly. Unannounced, however, the end will create curiosity and will have a stronger impact – if it really is a spectacular close.

6 As you want to leave a last positive impression on the participants, you should also end on a positive note. Even if your presentation deals with an unpleasant subject, your conclusion has to create hope, make the participants feel good and provoke a positive response. A disastrous drop in turnover? Yes, but the tone of your conclusion has to be, 'We will turn things round'. Never end on a negative note! Imagine the Chairman of the Board saying at the end of his presentation about the organization's bad financial situation, 'I'm afraid that's the way it looks. Not much scope for optimism. That's all I have to say'. You and every other participant would leave the room feeling depressed. No positive appeal, no hope, no uniting conclusion. You feel totally alone. The expression 'Good luck' is *not* a conclusion, it is an empty phrase. Those who finish with 'That's about it' or 'Good luck' end without an ending.

7 Some speakers tend to become pompous at the end of their speech: 'May the future ...', 'May this never again ...' or, 'This great company of ours ...'. Not even clergymen end their sermons with a dramatic 'may' any more.

8 'I could say a lot more on this subject, but ...'. Why on earth doesn't the speaker say it then?! Have they planned the presentation wrongly? This is just one more example of a bad ending.

9 'Unfortunately time has run out...'. Speakers often underestimate how long their speech will take to present. They suddenly look at their watches and realize that they have spoken far too long already. The speaker panics; the participants start to get restless and the conclusion – which might have been well-prepared originally – is cut and the speech is broken off hastily. What remains is a bad impression. You can avoid bad time-planning by preparing as described and checking your watch regularly.

10 No ending. Speakers leave it up to chance and then don't find one.

HOW TO END ON THE RIGHT NOTE

After these examples of how *not* to finish your speech we next have 15 techniques for concluding your speech well. Please bear in mind, however, that every speech needs its *own* ending, tailored to its content, the participants and the atmosphere. The list therefore gives you a broad spectrum of possibilities. Choosing the right one is up to you. It is important to understand the principle, rather than just copy an ending.

> A successful speech should enrich and its conclusion should reinforce its impact. The following examples show you how.

1 'In one word', 'To conclude', 'As a final point', 'And finally'

These phrases make it clear to everyone – even to those who did not pay attention throughout the entire speech – that now we are coming to the end. And then comes the conclusion, maybe best in a single sentence. For example, 'This has been a fantastic financial year!' or, 'We are number one – and we will remain so', or, 'Our concept works, even in the current economic climate'.

2 Summary in three points

A brief summary is a good ending. You give the participants the impression that your presentation is clearly structured and conclusive, that you have said everything that is important and only want to remind them of the essential points. This makes it easy for the participants. But, have no more than three points! If you present more, the summary will lose clarity and impact. Here are three examples of this principle in action, appropriately enough:

- *'The three most important elements of our business are research, development and customer service.'*

- *'Our product philosophy can thus be expressed in three words: sun, air and light!'*

- *'The three most important decisions are, first, to target the market of single mothers more intensively. Second, to hold our position in the market segment of bachelors. And, third, aim with all means available, to win the market segment of the older generation, which we have so far neglected.'*

3 Vision of the future

'These crucial changes will help us to really master the future.' Looking ahead, and thus, into the future, lends more weight to your statements. 'And from now on we will show a warmer, friendlier attitude towards our customers.' Of course, this looking ahead should be positive and full of optimism. Another example, 'When we meet again in four months' time we will already have accomplished 30 per cent of the task we have set ourselves today'.

4 Practical benefits

'This method will help you achieve the following:...' Your participants' expectations are at the heart of your communication. The participants want to know what consequences your speech has for them. 'With the help of these tools we can start simplifying our order intake procedure immediately.' 'But what's in it for me?', the participants ask themselves. As a good communicator, you tell them once more in your conclusion: 'Increasing productivity by 10 per cent – for you that means job security, higher income and social benefits'. This also transfers your statements from a purely factual sphere to a more direct, motivating level.

5 Using the start of your speech

'At the beginning, we decided that we will have to change our strategy – and we have not only found a new strategy, we have also taken the first step towards implementing it.' Using the beginning of a speech is a very elegant way of concluding it. You thus complete the circle, bringing the end of your presentation round to its beginning. The Marketing Manager of a spectacles manufacturer says to the assembled department stores' buyers, 'At the beginning of my presentation I asked whether you knew that one in four people are short-sighted. What you also now know is that every other optician suffers from short-sightedness of a different kind. This is your chance. Use it!' 'At the beginning we were faced with a decision. You said "Yes" to it. Now we must start putting this decision into practice,' the Production Manager tells the engineers.

6 The IBP turned round or repeated, moving the promise of benefits to the end

'Ten new ideas are what we promised you at the beginning. Ten new ideas are what you have heard. If you use only *three* of them, it will have been worth your while attending today', concludes the Director of a marketing agency in a presentation to the agency's staff. This is a good ending, going back to the attention-grabbing promise of benefits at the beginning of the speech and fulfilling it. It is thus a renewed appeal to the participants' motivation. 'And the final, positive note is: this is the way ahead. All you have to do is put into practice what you have worked out in these two hours today.' The initial benefit promise can also be turned into a final benefit promise. For example, 'When you apply this approach to your next sales negotiation, you will realize how much easier it becomes'.

7 Appeal

'We can continue to expand our market share. To achieve this, each of us has to act on what we decided today. So, let's begin right now.' Good communicators, who are able to motivate their participants, choose sentences with a clear appeal as their conclusion, to get spontaneous agreement or action. Politicians do that before elections: 'There is no alternative: vote for us', 'That is why: let's go and do it!', 'Purely understanding the situation won't get us anywhere. We must act'.

8 A surprising conclusion

During a press visit to the Far East, the Chief Executive of a large computer firm surprised the journalists at the end of his speech with the words, 'To conclude this presentation, here is some remarkable news for you. An hour ago, we managed to win an order worth over £40 million in the face of stiff American competition. And you are the first people to hear about it'. Such surprise endings must be well stage-managed to create an excellent final impact. A surprising conclusion can help create a dramatic peak to raise the value of even a mediocre speech. The participants at an event will certainly be pleasantly surprised when the speaker suddenly says, 'And now, ten minutes earlier than expected, we can close this session. Take a brief look at the last page of your documentation. Do you agree with these simple measures. Yes? Good.'

9 Creating a feeling of success, appealing to joint achievements

'We have found more ideas we can use in this meeting than ever before. We can really be pleased with ourselves.' Joint achievements are a basis on which you can easily build a bridge to your participants. Be careful, however, when using the notion 'we are all in the same boat' – don't be too flippant with it, too pally. And only address common ground that is really there. Another good ending is to emphasize the success of a meeting as being the success of the whole group by saying, 'In three hours we have managed to prepare a completely new budget, which reduces our costs by 10 per cent. That's what you can call *true* creativity'.

10 A genuine thank you (for commitment)

At the end you can also say thank you – not for listening, but for the achievements of the participants: 'Let me finish by thanking you very much for your contributions, your ideas – and, most of all, for your commitment'. You can also go one step further and praise past performance. If a department has shown particular commitment over the past quarter and performed very well, you can praise them in front of all the participants: 'Thank you very much for your remarkable commitment, your exceptional performance and magnificent results. Keep it up! We shall try to do the same'. A last sentence like this will stick in the minds of the participants.

11 'One last thought ...'

Do not introduce new ideas in the last few sentences of a speech! If, exceptionally, you still want to do it – perhaps because the questions asked by the participants have shown that you have neglected a certain point or because you want to particularly highlight one major thought, you should give it special emphasis: 'One last thought ... . Allow yourself to...'. You can use this to reinforce the impact of your presentation and to motivate accordingly. It acts like a P.S. at the end of a letter. 'And now, one final suggestion: start implementing your action programme from tomorrow, the first day in your future professional career.'

12 Primary appeals – appeal to the heart, not the mind

Head or heart? Mind or emotions? Which are easier to appeal to? Participants always react more quickly and more lastingly to appeals that play on their emotions rather than to factual, reason-based arguments. A good speaker takes advantage of this by choosing an emotional ending: 'We can be successful, reach our goals, achieve more than we ever hoped for. Profit is not only beneficial to business, it also boosts your position.' Compare Chapter 14 on the subject of primary appeals.

13 The highlight of your speech: using a crescendo to intensify your finish

The conclusion of your speech has to be intensified. It must be different to the other parts of the speech, especially in its expression. The close must be the highlight of your performance, its dramatic peak. Thus, lower your voice beforehand, mobilize your reserves of strength, bring your entire conviction to bear and intensify your expression. Remember, don't lower your voice in the last sentence, otherwise half your impact is lost.

14 Adding 'we' to primary appeals

The conclusion should end with a feeling that common ground has been shared. That's why 'we' is better than 'you'. For example, 'Now we are at the top. Let us remain here. We will all benefit from it'. The list of primary appeals in Chapter 14 shows you the various possibilities.

15 Using the good openings

Go back a few pages! In the previous chapter, you will find several approaches that also make a good conclusion.

When you have tested your conclusion and established that it really is the optimal one, learn the last few sentences by heart. They are so crucial to the effect of your entire speech, they must be perfect. This applies to the first and the last sentences of your speech, but *only* to them! **Learn them by heart!**

> **And now you will be able to answer the four questions and solve the four problems at the beginning of this chapter!**

The conclusion, then, is the highlight of your speech, your final burst. Plan it well and practise it. The last sentence must come out perfectly. And it must be memorable. It is the last impression you leave with your participants.

8

PAY CLOSE ATTENTION TO ORGANIZATIONAL DETAILS

Can you answer the following four questions?

1 Can mistakes in the organization of an event lead to a total failure in your communication with participants?

2 Can the seating order be of crucial importance?

3 What do you do with a small number of participants spread out in a large room?

4 Which logistical points have to be checked in order to safeguard the smooth running of an event?

Can you solve the following four problems?

1 Richard Bernhard, a German management consultant, has to give a presentation to a group of company directors in Stockholm. He is advised to speak in English as the participants understand English better than German. Although he speaks English well, he hesitates because he feels he cannot express himself as effectively in English as in his mother tongue. He asks whether or not it would be possible to have his German presentation translated into Swedish by an interpreter, which, according to him, would be in everyone's best interest. He knows nothing about the number of participants or the composition of the group. He does not know their expectations, how many of them speak German or whether there are facilities for simultaneous translation.

What do you think? What would you advise him to do?

_____

_____

_____

_____

2 Two speakers discuss whether or not to distribute handouts before or after the event. There are good arguments in favour of both options. One of the speakers decides to distribute her handouts to the participants before giving her presentation. The second speaker prefers to distribute them after his speech. Both speakers are moderately successful. In the case of the first speaker, the participants understand the presentation well and easily, but it doesn't grab them; whereas the second speaker comes across as a strong presenter. The participants understand the second speaker, but later on they cannot really remember what had been said.

Which option do you think is the more appropriate one? Is there a third one?

_____

_____

_____

_____

3 At a large congress, one of the presentations takes place in the restaurant. The lighting in the room is a bit low. The company's current TV advertisements are projected on to a large screen. Messages from absent members of the Board are then read out.

Immediately after dinner, several speakers, who are all seated on the platform, get up one after the other to talk. During the speeches, waiters clear the tables. Now and then, there are announcements about apparently important telephone calls.

Make a list of the mistakes made

_____

_____

_____

_____

_____

_____

4 Glen Bishop has prepared everything to a tee. He has practised his speech, spent a lot of time on its format and content – and has brought several plants into the village hall to illustrate his presentation on the flora and fauna of his native village. He has also managed to get hold of a slide projector. He tries out the projector beforehand to make sure it works, which it does. During the presentation, however, the bulb in the projector, which had worked fine during the rehearsal, explodes with a loud bang – and a spare one is not to be found anywhere. The presentation has to be interrupted several times and, finally, has to be curtailed. Whether or not the 200 participants will bother coming back to the second meeting is anyone's guess.

What does this episode teach us – apart from the importance of spare bulbs?

_____

_____

_____

BE PREPARED!

Lord Baden-Powell was famous for his motto – 'Be prepared', abbreviated to 'BP'. Being prepared and being ready was the most important thing for the man who founded the boy scout movement in 1908. The same should also apply to good communicators. This includes all the practical arrangements. If not, it doesn't matter how well you prepare your speech – the event is still likely to fail.

> **Organizational defects, even trivial matters, can destroy the best speech!**

Many speakers have slipped up due to 'trivial matters'. The manager of an international advertising agency forgot to test the microphone before her presentation to an important client. During her speech, the microphone vibrated so badly that her voice was completely distorted and could not be heard at all for a few seconds. Although an in-house technician was there immediately to repair the defect, she was so completely thrown by this that she lost her thread, forgot all her good points and stumbled through the presentation like a complete beginner. In addition, she realized that her transparencies with all the important figures on them were illegible because they were too small. She had well and truly blown her presentation. Everyone showed sympathetic understanding about the mishaps that caused her loss of confidence, but the major client signed a contract with another agency.

What can you learn from this? If you have to (or want to) use visual aids, test them beforehand! Not just once, but at least twice. And always have a technician on stand-by during your presentation. Choose a microphone that can be clipped to you or hung round your neck. Would you like to learn something about microphone technology? You don't need to. It is not you that has to adapt to the technology, the technology has to adapt to *you*. The only thing you have to worry about is that the volume is not set too low. When you test it, bear in mind that your voice will always sound louder in an empty room than in a full one. Don't strain your voice too much or you will tire quickly. If in doubt, always use a microphone, even if people suggest that you don't need one.

That is only one example of what can happen. There are numerous examples of speakers who stumble over organizational flaws – and do not recover. As everyone knows, prevention is better than cure. If you follow the basic rules given in this chapter, nothing should happen – from an organizational point of view – to jeopardize your speech. Of course, you can delegate some of these measures to an assistant, but have them work under your supervision. You are the boss. Arrangements that suit others ('The Prime Minister has spoken here before and he thought the set-up was fine') can seriously harm you. The organization has to be right for *you*.

PRACTICAL ORGANIZATIONAL ARRANGEMENTS

1 Use a checklist to be on the safe side

Put together a checklist before every event and go through it point by point *on site*. These things you need to check are all small, but paying attention to detail at the outset saves you lots of headaches later. From the dimensions of the speaker's platform, to the various pieces of technical equipment and to the seating order of the participants, check them all – don't underestimate them. They could make the difference between your success and failure.

2 Choice of room

Try to influence the set-up of your 'playing field'. You are the speaker, the most important person. Your concern is successful communication. If the organizer of the event has chosen the room and the acoustics are bad, the tables are arranged the wrong way round (short side to the front, for example) and the light conditions are unsatisfactory, then you have to change that. Check the room conditions in good time and lend a hand yourself to improve things as necessary if helpers are unavailable. Small rooms are better than large ones (they enable you to be closer to the participants), natural light is better than artificial light (it is less tiring). Is there any noise from outside (traffic or disturbing music)? Are there any vision-impairing columns? How does the air-conditioning work? And don't, under any circumstances, choose a cinema or theatre – they are too comfortable, dark and muffle sound and the platform (stage) is remote from the audience.

3 The setting or 'atmosphere'

Choosing the right setting also contributes to the success or failure of your presentation. If you want to call on the participants of an event to take part in a demonstration against the destruction of the environment, the event should not be organized at a private club or a smart hotel. Conversely, a celebration held in honour of long-serving members of staff should not be held in a school hall. Restaurants are only really suitable for after-dinner speeches.

Take care that the 'climate' is right, too – that the participants aren't racing from another presentation to yours or are still fired up after a previous debate when you are ready to address a completely different subject. Flowers enhance the atmosphere. So do pictures, banners, exhibits, photographic displays, small gifts on the seats and music during breaks.

4 Seating order

This concerns the seating plan for the chairman, guests and grouping of participants. It has to be organized. Never leave it to chance where your supporters and potential opponents are seated. Divide the participants according to your interests. Otherwise, it may happen that unimportant participants are sitting in the first few rows, while your special guests have to stand.

If the room chosen turns out to be too big, because instead of the 200 people expected only 50 show up, make them sit in the rows at the front. That way the few participants won't look so lost in the large room.

Putting the committee on the platform has become a bad habit – it only flatters the egos of the few concerned. A place in the front row would be just as appropriate and would be less intrusive.

Regarding guests of honour, usually fewer will come than expected and empty places in the front row disrupt the seating arrangements and create embarrassment. Don't reserve seats, but, instead, supply a comfortable chair for each guest of honour on their arrival. And what about the public welcome? A really outstanding guest of honour should, of course, be welcomed by name; half a dozen or more of them however should not. Why not? Because where do you start? Where do you end? It could cause ill-feelings among those omitted. A friendly, general welcome greeting is less risky – and less time-consuming.

5 Audio-visual aids

Check your microphone, transparencies, slides – make sure they are legible! Also, the platform speaker's lectern, etc. Check everything, twice! Make sure you always have replacement bulbs, spare transparencies, pens and a spare projector. You never know!

You need audio-visual aids to communicate successfully, but they have to be used correctly. Do you recognize the following situation? A speaker has put a transparency on the overhead projector and wants to point at something on it. He stands in front of the screen, uses his fingers and obscures part of the illustration; maybe he even turns his back on the participants. A second example. The transparency you are using to illustrate the decline in turnover has to be legible not only to people in the front row but also to those at the very back. There is a rule of thumb for the size the characters need to be to ensure this:

- up to a distance of 10 metres (11 yards) the letters have to be at least 5 millimetres ($^3/_{16}$ inch) high.

- 10 to 15 metres (11 to 16$^1/_2$ yards) away, 10 millimetres ($^3/_8$ inch)

- 15 to 20 metres (16$^1/_2$ to 22 yards) 15 millimetres ($^5/_8$ inch)

- 20 to 25 metres (22 to 27$^1/_3$ yards) 20 millimetres ($^{13}/_{16}$ inch)

- 30 metres (33 yards), 25 millimetres (1 inch).

The following rules apply to the use of audio-visual aids:

- use only material that everyone can see

- prepare it very well

- have everything to hand (number the items!)

- explain them correctly when necessary

- limit the number of slides: your speech should not be a slide-show, but a communication!

- get experts to create illustrations, pictures, slides – text alone is not enough!

- involve the participants – 'Can you read this bit here?', 'You might want to copy this down'.

6 Lighting and ventilation

The room should not be darkened because the participants will want to take notes; you want them to participate actively, and you want to control them. Even if the slides don't look as bright, leave the light on. If the lighting is too dim, the participants will fall asleep! If it glares it will cause weariness, resulting in watery eyes and headaches. Thus, check the lighting – the amount and direction. What is the air like?

Open the windows to ventilate the room and do this again just before your presentation. Switch any air-conditioning on early enough. If the air is hot and stuffy, not even the most promising communication will work.

7 Clothing

Is there a dress code? This is something you have to find out in advance. Imagine you are going to speak at a five-star international hotel in front of a group of merchant bankers. The invitation asks for business attire and you arrive in jeans. You might not even be allowed into the hotel – despite the fact that you are the main speaker at the event.

Another point: it is not only TV presenters who have to be aware of the studio background; any speaker should do the same. You are talking at the annual shareholders' meeting in front of 3000 people. Perhaps the wall behind the lectern is dark blue; so is your suit. Do you think that participants sitting in the back row will be able to see you? People will pay better attention to you if you stand out against the background.

8 The time plan, sequence of events, breaks, refreshments and smoking

All these points have to be indicated in the programme or agenda. If you as Chairman of the Board have to announce bad news at a shareholders' meeting, for example, wait until after lunch or dinner, if possible – and make sure that the food and drinks are good. It will help to calm their minds. You can even offer a cold buffet during an event on the shop floor. Full mouths complain less loudly and full stomachs are less likely to rebel.

Last and by no means least, include sufficient breaks in your programme, especially with a view to accommodating smokers. If smoking is prohibited during the event (which is quite common nowadays), they will become fidgety and pay less attention after one hour at the most.

9 Speaking order

If you have an influence on the speaking order (and you will have in nine out of ten cases), you should not speak around lunch time. At about 2 p.m. the ability to concentrate is particularly low. Try to be the first speaker. That way you can get it over and done with and you don't risk repeating what the previous speakers have said or suffer from the effect of their possibly bad speeches. The later your turn is, the harder it becomes for you to gain and maintain attention.

10 Additional points

- Don't keep drinking during your speech! One of the participants may call out 'Cheers', which will make everyone laugh, but at your expense!

- Via the microphone, everyone can hear you swallow. Not very pleasant.

- Don't, under any circumstances, smoke during your presentation – not even at informal events. You will lose the support of your participants.

- Agree a sign language with your assistant to stage manage the event (including the timing of your speech, special instructions, etc.) Make them give you a five-minute warning before the end of your speech.

- Take a lectern along. Having your script on the table in front of you prevents eye contact. Fixed lecterns are generally not suited to the light or your eye sight. Follow the checklist on page 94 and the previous ten points above. It will cost you some time, but if you don't do it, it will cost you nerves and, possibly, failure. Trivial points can ruin the best speech.

  Consider the subject of the translation or interpretation of speeches abroad or in front of foreign visitors. You may feel that using a foreign language is a considerable obstacle. You shouldn't feel this way. It provides you with three advantages:

  - it will automatically win you everyone's support and they will like you for it

- you will express yourself very simply as, understandably, you can't do it any other way

- participants will be more than willing to help you out should you have any difficulties, which creates spontaneous AP, leading to genuine dialogue.

If you don't know a certain word, ask. There are speakers who consciously use their language handicap to win them goodwill and make them likeable to the participants. Even in a language completely unknown to you, you can learn a few words by heart and use them at the beginning of your speech. Translations and interpreters are always a disadvantage, even though they are sometimes unavoidable. Bear the following in mind: if there is no simultaneous translation, you will lose at least half of your speaking time. Always run through your speech – especially technical words – with the interpreters, well in advance. Whichever mode is used, you will have to slow down your habitual rhythm.

On the subject of distributing handouts (for presentations with important information content), give them out:

- beforehand if comprehension is more important than effect

- afterwards if the effect of your presentation is more important than is correctly absorbing the information

- during if it is possible to combine both methods and you wish to add some variety and create a special effect.

These last two methods allow you greater flexibility; you can leave things out or amend them.

> And now you can answer the four introductory questions and solve the four organizational problems, right?

Are you convinced now? Trivial organizational matters *can* completely ruin your speech. So, take care of the content and form of your presentation and organizational issues. It may be tedious, but it is absolutely necessary.

CHECKLIST FOR PRESENTATIONS TO LARGE GROUPS

Podium

- *Area:* 2 to 3 square metres ($2^{1/3}$ to $3^{1/2}$ square yards)

- *Height* 30 to 60 centimetres (12 to $23^{1/2}$ inches).

- Preferably covered with carpet and/or cloth.

Lectern

- A desktop lectern on a solid table surface is better than a free-standing lectern. Place it at a comfortable reading height (put a lip at the bottom edge to keep your papers from slipping).

- Cover the lower part of the table with a cloth, to hide your legs.

- Don't use a lamp (it can be blinding); good room lighting is adequate.

Overhead projector

- A transparency roll (make sure it is clean and does not run out during the event) is better than loose transparencies.

- Place the projector to the right of the lectern if you are right-handed, to the left if you are left-handed (check it is quiet, produces a sharp image and matches the size of the screen).

- Have five or more spare pens.

- Have an additional roll of film.

Projector screen

- Check that the typeface of your transparencies is large enough to be legible from everywhere in the room.

- Place it behind the speaker (check that the images are clearly visible and sharp, even from the last rows).

- Project the transparency centrally on the screen.

- Don't darken the room, even if the image projected is then not quite as bright.

Table

- Ensure it is solid, 50 to 60 centimetres (20 to $23\frac{1}{2}$ inches) behind the lectern, so you can lean on it (also useful for putting your papers on once you've finished with them).

Microphone

- Ideally, use a cordless microphone clipped to your clothes, to allow you freedom of movement. Otherwise use a microphone that hangs round your neck with a 6-metre ($6\frac{1}{2}$-yard) cord.

Technician

- One should always be present in order to repair any possible faults or breakdowns quickly.

Assistant

- Ditto. Could be a colleague, secretary or a friend (to help with other unexpected problems.

Lighting	• A maximum amount of natural light.
Temperature	• Between 16 and 18°C (60 to 64°F) at the start – the room will warm up automatically once the participants have arrived; have it checked regularly
	• Open windows during each break, to allow fresh air in.
Smoking ban	• Apply it, but put friendly signs at the room entrance and place ash trays there (and only there).
Bell	• To signal the end of breaks.
Question box	• Put it in a clearly visible place and label it – for those who would prefer to write down their questions.
Break room	• Well separated from the room in which you are making the presentation to give you the opportunity to withdraw during the breaks.
Doors	• Always have them supervised to avoid interruptions (people entering and leaving).
Telephone calls	• Don't let them interrupt the presentation. Have messages taken for participants for them to collect from near the room entrance or at the conference desk during break times.
Refreshments	• Have soft drinks and a coffee/tea bar and ensure quick service.

Seating order

- Participants should sit as closely as possible to the speaker's platform.

- Use the width of the room, if possible, rather than its length.

- Arrange tables in a herringbone pattern (covered with cloths, but not white ones).

- Fill the front seats first. Have all seats at the back roped off with 'reserved' signs, usher people forwards, then take off the signs when the room fills up.

- If possible encourage people to change seats at longer events as this creates movement and livelier contacts between participants.

- Introduce controlled, brief 'leg stretcher' breaks.

- Remember, with larger groups, everything needs to be amplified – presentation, projection, EVA (eyes, voice, attitude), liveliness, visuals, jokes, spectacular attention getters and, last, but not least, your control of the event.

9

CONTROL YOUR STAGE FRIGHT

Can you answer the following four questions?

1 Do even experienced speakers, politicians and actors suffer from stage fright? All of them? Some? None?

2 Does stage fright have a mainly paralysing or mainly stimulating effect?

3 Should you take tranquillizers if you suffer from excessive stage fright?

4 Are there any tricks to help you avoid stage fright?

Can you solve the following four problems?

1 Sarah Brown is the Training Manager in a large construction machinery manufacturer. She considers herself to be an experienced speaker. Sarah regularly gives presentations to both apprentices and heads of department in her company. She claims, 'I don't suffer from stage fright any more, I got over that a long time ago.' During her attendance at a seminar entitled 'Communication Skills for Top Executives', the seminar leader assesses her as 'quite a good speaker, but, right now, at best a mediocre communicator'.

Can you work out what qualities Sarah Brown lacks?

_____

_____

_____

2 Michel Leclerc is Director of Science and Technology for a pharmaceutical company, and is also responsible for the technical training of
the firm's pharmacists. For years, he has been giving the same lecture
on the tolerance of certain drugs at pharmacists' association meetings.
He obviously experiences no stage fright. One day, he is interrupted
during his speech. One of the participants asks him an unforeseen,
tricky question. Michel is completely thrown by this, starts to stutter
and loses his thread – and this is aggravated further after another, albeit
harmless, question. This had never happened to him when speaking at
internal meetings in front of his colleagues.

**Was it a mistake to allow questions at all? And was it an omission
not to have been prepared for this specific question? What was the
main stress factor for Michel in this situation?**

---

3 'I've known the symptoms for years. The day before an important
lecture I start suffering from a mild headache. A few hours before the
actual event, the pain gets so bad that I have to take a tablet. In order to
be alert and responsive during my speech and the discussion afterwards, I usually have a small whisky or two immediately before speaking. I know that this isn't good, but it helps me to keep calm.'

Does it really help? What would you recommend doing instead?

---

4 On the third day of a congress on environmental protection, at 8 a.m., Dr Nils Repen, Director of Application Technology for a chemical firm, gives a speech on the dangers of the destruction of the ozone layer. Nils is a very conscientious person. He has participated in the whole event, listened attentively to all the lectures and noted everything down carefully. For business reasons, he also attended the banquet on the second evening of the event, which went on until late in the night. When a colleague suggested that maybe he should go to bed a bit earlier in view of the fact that he was giving a speech the next morning, he replied 'I don't mind a late night – I can easily cope with that'. The next morning, he realizes that he can't find the right words for a proper beginning; that he is unable to answer questions as quickly as usual, and that, overall, he feels more irritable than normal.

Maybe he had taken on too much after all? Did he really have to participate in everything?

THE POSITIVE SIDE OF STAGE FRIGHT

Let me say one thing to start with: every good speaker suffers from stage fright! Some more, some less. Neither the TV presenter who looks in control, nor the politician radiating self-confidence, nor the brilliant historian are calm inside when they step in front of the camera or on to the speaker's platform. And that is a good thing. Let us find out why.

Everyone has experiences of stage fright. We suffered from it as children having to recite a poem at Christmas, before the first presentation in class, then during A levels, college exams and, later on, before job interviews. Stage fright is very natural. If you control it, it is more of a help than an obstacle. You don't believe it? Read this chapter – and you will see what I mean.

'Stage fright is nervousness or panic that may beset a person about to appear in front of an audience.' That is how a dictionary defines it. Stage fright is the fear of failure. Yet this fear is a very natural consequence of placing high demands on yourself, especially at important events. Hopefully you have such ambitions. Only people who don't care whether their performance is good or bad or about the impact they have on others have no stage fright. Should they really be allowed to appear in front of a public at all? At the other extreme are those who suffer terribly from stage fright – the perfectionists, who hate even the smallest mistake or irregularity. Thus, no ambitions, no stage fright; high ambition, severe stage fright.

Examine yourself. If you suffer from stage fright before public appearances, speeches, receptions, lectures or discussions, it's a positive sign – it means that you expect and demand something of yourself. You want to be up to the task you are facing.

So, we agree, stage fright is a positive thing! Now you will argue, 'That is very interesting, but what's the benefit if it nearly paralyses me?' You will see. What you are about to find out about stage fright will help you, especially if you follow the recommendations given.

The symptoms of stage fright are numerous. Everyone experiences this nervousness and tension differently. One person may get a trembling voice or lose it altogether, another keeps looking at the floor or the ceiling for fear and a third doesn't even recognize their best friends! The pulse rate, which is normally between 60 and 80, shoots up to 130, 140 or even 150 at the beginning of a speech. This is an extreme strain that can only be compared with other extreme situations. Pulse rates of up to 200 have been recorded in racing drivers, for example. It creates stress, but stress can be positive.

That is why a good opening to a speech is so important. An effective start – for example successful AP, which gives you immediate feedback – helps you lose your stage fright and gain real self-confidence. That brings us on to the tips and tricks you can use to control stage fright. First of all, follow these four pieces of advice and you will enter the fray with a lot more confidence.

1 How often have I rehearsed the speech out loud during my preparation?

Certainly not often enough. You cannot do it often enough before 'the real thing'. Many speakers think it is silly, practising a speech aloud again and again. Yet, experience shows that only when you hear your-self speak will you notice the rough edges that have to be smoothed out, that the emphases need to be changed, that it needs to be made more fluent. When you have done this, you gain confidence and are in the right mood for your presentation. If you are embarrassed about talk-ing aloud in the office, go to a park at lunch time or book a meeting room. Did you know that both Churchill and de Gaulle used to rehearse their speeches in front of a mirror?

2 Practise early

You read in Chapter 1 that preparing early and well means you are halfway there. Almost all speakers start rehearsing their speeches too late. The time you spend rehearsing well ahead of time is a real invest-ment. The benefits are less stage fright and the applause from your par-ticipants.

3 Switch off before switching on

Sportsmen and women prepare for an event by retreating into a training camp to switch off. Immediately before competing, they practically shut the world out altogether. Do the same. Withdraw for an hour to build up your strength in peace. Alternatively, do some light exercise, have some fun and take your mind off the presentation. Most impor-tantly, get some fresh air. When you are well-rested you will be more confident and concentrate better. In turn, you will be able to react better and be more convincing. So, switch off before switching on your speech!

4 What you do in the last few hours and minutes before your speech can influence your stage fright

Things you shouldn't do: mental work (burdens your mind), go on lonely walks (you can't switch off then), take part in the whole event (like a congress) before your own speech. What you should do: eat light food, have no alcohol and get an early night. After all, you want to be able to perform. And, another tip (copied from sportsmen and actors): do relaxing exercises, stretching, tighten-release sequences of muscle movements, shout, gesticulate, laugh, whistle – psyche yourself up.

When you are about to speak, make contact with the participants even before you start. Talk to them, shake hands, greet people you know, bring along friends to encourage you. The more you communicate with the participants beforehand, by asking questions and giving answers, approaching them and mixing with them, the more you will lose your stage fright. Try it!

> **Treat stage fright as a natural occurrence – it mobilizes your reserves and makes you alert and ready to perform.**

Your answers to the questionnaire opposite will help you to get your stage fright under control and to change the negative into the positive. What do you do if you get stuck in the middle of your speech? Many speakers are afraid of losing their thread during a presentation. Fear paralyses! And fear leads to stage fright. If you know what to do in case you get stuck, you will lose your fear (on pages 108 to 110 you will find 12 tips on how to get out of these situations).

How about interruptions? First, prepare yourself for all likely disruptions and think about how to handle them. Try to put up with the unavoidable ones calmly. Ask an assistant to help deal with all types of interruptions, ranging from a participant's hiccups to telephone calls, people entering and leaving or speaking to each other, acoustic mishaps and other unintentional disruptions.

Second, pre-empt potential restlessness on the part of participants by having short breaks, stop repeated disruptions decisively and ignore what you can't change (more on this subject in Chapter 13).

TEN QUESTIONS TO OVERCOME STAGE FRIGHT

If your answers are mainly 'No's', this is a concrete warning of strong, negative stage fright. If this is the case, take action to succeed in your task.

	Yes	No	Action
1 Have I chosen the 'right' subject? Does the subject suit me? Do I know it well enough? Does it correspond to the participants' EMMA? Does it fit the occasion?			
2 Have I prepared early enough and in the right way? **Have I tested my presentation of it?** **Am I on form?** How early? How thoroughly? How does it sound at the dress rehearsal? Am I : • well-rested? • fit? • optimistic? • looking forward to the occasion?			

	Yes	No	Action
3 Do I talk instead of 'giving a speech'? Do I avoid unnecessary strain? Do I avoid using 'I'? Am I expressing myself in my normal everyday language? Would I talk to my best friends like this? Am I avoiding complicated trains of thoughts and expressions? Am I constantly saying 'You' or 'We'?			
4 Have I got the right key word noted down to avoid losing my train of thought? Is the layout clear? Are my notes easy to read? Written clearly? Are they brief notes only – headlines, not whole sentences?			
5 Do I use every opportunity to elicit feedback (activity, contact with listeners, voice, eye contact, group control, shorter distance, participation)? Do I shake hands beforehand? Is the distance to the nearest participant short? Do I speak loudly? Do I speak slowly? Do I ensure my eyes are wandering, involving everyone? Do I create frequent AP?			
6 Have I checked all the equipment again? All the items? The microphone too? Pens? Papers?			

	Yes	No	Action
Legibility? Lighting? Air? Timing?			
7 Am I using the right tactics to help me over the opening 30–50 seconds (silence, mock beginning, quotations, questions, reading from script, learning by heart, contact with participants?)			
Do I only start once the group is totally silent?			
Do I interrupt immediately at the first sign of noise?			
Do I use possible mock (fake) beginnings: 'Ladies and gentlemen' – interruption, then, when everybody is silent, the real beginning?			
Do I read the first few sentences from my script?			
Do I manage to instantly involve or activate the participants?			
8 Do I consciously try to make my job easier (short sentences, pauses, correct breathing)?			
Such as leaving out unnecessary words?			
Avoiding long, complicated sentences?			
More pauses between the sentences (a rest for myself as well as the participants)?			
Do I take the time to breathe calmly?			
Do I consciously loosen up my tense posture?			
9 Do I act like a 'winner' (smile, speak confidently, take the bull by the horns)?			
Do I avoid showing a lack of confidence?			

	Yes	No	Action
Do I show a friendly smile when meeting difficulties?			
Do I cover up inhibitions and insecurity? Do I avoid admitting to them?			
Do I hide whatever fear I have from everyone?			
Do I remember that *acting* like a winner will *make* me a winner?			
10 Do I think like a winner?			
Do I think of success, rather than failure?			
Do I repeatedly say to myself 'I'm going to do it'?			
Do I consciously ban negative thoughts from my mind?			
Do I see participants as positive, interested people?			
Do I say to myself 'I wouldn't be scared of them as individuals, so why should I be scared of them as a group?'			

WHAT TO DO WHEN YOU LOSE YOUR THREAD

If you get stuck in the middle of a speech – and it happens to everyone – there is no need to wish the earth would open up beneath your feet. There are 12 ways to avoid 'getting stuck', and thus reduce the risk of negative stage fright taking over.

1 Introduce the forgotten thought later on

Ignore the hole in your train of thought. If you carry on with the point after the one you have forgotten, then you will, at some stage, remember where you got stuck. You can then add in that point, by saying, for example, 'By the way ...'. If not, leave it out!

2 Leave out the thought altogether

How would the participants notice that you have omitted a point? After all, they don't know your manuscript, do they?

3 Announce that the point will be discussed later on

'We will get back to this point later,' and add 'if we have the time...'. That is one way to get over the mishap. If you then still can't remember the point, the participants will probably have forgotten about it as well. Besides, you may run out of time at the end anyway.

4 Go into freewheeling mode, just talking

Many speakers are too good at this – they hardly do anything else but speak without saying anything. *You* should only use it as a last resort, in an emergency. No one will notice. If you can't remember your next point, bridge the gap with set phrases, empty words, repetition, redundancies until you have found a good thought. Doing this is far better than pausing, which will paralyse you.

5 'You know what I mean ...'

Foreign words and technical expressions, but many ordinary words as well, often block speakers – they get stuck. So, why not use simpler, more common words in the first place? If you get stuck in the middle of a complicated expression, you are bound to get a laugh if you say, 'Oh, you know what I mean ... '. The participants will gladly empathize with you.

6 Recap on your last thought

This is another way to save yourself. Simply create a 'loop' in your speech. Maybe the elusive next point will occur to you while you say 'once again …', or, 'just briefly …'.

7 Buy yourself time

An elegant way of covering up the fact that you've lost your thread is to say, for example, 'Maybe you should take a few notes here', or, 'Are there any questions?' Prepared questions are also very useful: 'You might ask yourself ...', or, 'What are your thoughts on this?'

8 Take a break

If you get stuck, just say: 'Let's have a short break now to stretch our legs. We will continue in five minutes'.

9 Never admit you are lost

Admitting it *is* honest, but it will not earn you any brownie points. The participants will interpret it as a weakness on your part. It would be better to use point 10, instead.

10 'Let's go on to point X'

Simply continue your speech with the next point. Don't be disappointed – people just won't notice.

11 Get the participants to fill the gap

'We've mentioned two points so far. What do you think will be the third one?' This way you hand the problem over to your participants, win time and achieve excellent AP, as well as attention and cooperation.

12 Other possibilities

Here are just three:

- summarise: 'So far we have heard ...'

- provide a technical fault – pretend the projector has just broken down, the microphone has failed, the screen has got stuck, the cord has broken – or deliberately cause a breakdown. (All of these are better than an embarrassing pause.)

- blow your nose or drink some water (many politicians are obviously very well aware of this trick – watch them use it!)

As you can see, there is always a solution. Getting stuck will therefore not make you nervous any more. Still tense? Don't worry, remember the motto below.

> **A good speaker always has some stage fright.**

You can get rid of paralysing nervousness by using the tips given in this chapter. What remains is positive excitement, which is a source of energy that makes you perform at your best. Furthermore, in the future, you won't have problems with getting stuck.

> **You should now be able to answer the four introductory questions and solve the four problems!**

10

CHOOSE THE RIGHT SPEECH

1. Occasion speeches

Can you answer the following four questions?

1 Which two target groups do you have to address at a celebration speech?

2 What do you say to a member of staff who is retiring in order to make it easier for them to leave?

3 Does the organizer of an event have to introduce the speaker or should that be left to the speaker?

4 How can an event be saved if the speaker misses the main point or gives a poor performance?

Can you solve the following four problems?

1 The owner of a German high-tech company, Robert Neumann, is visiting Silicon Valley in California to gather information on the latest technological developments and, at the same time, see if there would be a market for his own components over there. One evening, he is invited to an American businesspersons' club. After the cocktails, the Club Secretary taps on his glass. To the complete surprise of Robert Neumann, who is totally unprepared, he says, 'Our German visitor, Robert Neumann, would like to say a few words'.

How could Robert Neumann master the situation?

_____

_____

_____

2 You have been invited to speak at an evening seminar. When you discuss the event with the organizer, you are asked whether or not you will allow them to introduce you to the participants as an expert in your field and a brilliant speaker, from whom much can be learnt. The organizer says that they want to 'upgrade' you in the introduction, sell you as a unique person and make the participants curious about you.

You are flattered, but believe that such an introduction will raise the audience's expectations excessively and put you under enormous pressure. How do you react?

_____

_____

_____

3 While having lunch with several journalists, Nils Lindström, PR manager for a Scandinavian airline, is asked to give a short travel report about an exotic, little-known region in south-east Asia. He chats about his experiences in great detail and consistently focuses on his own role. He gives a lengthy description of how his long experience enabled him to cope with the country, its people and their customs.

Nils notices that the journalists' attention dwindles more and more, the longer he talks. He stops after 35 minutes. What has he overlooked?

_____

_____

_____

4 A company celebration is planned at a large coffee-roasting firm. Several long-standing members of staff are to receive awards. Kelly Sparks, a leading trade union representative, finds out just before the celebration is due to begin that she is expected to give a speech. She tries to get out of it, but without succeeding. After all, the Personnel Manager says, she has known most of the colleagues who are to receive awards for years. Listening to the speakers preceding her, Kelly realizes that everything she wanted to say has already been mentioned.

What would you do if you were in Kelly's shoes?

_____

_____

_____

WHAT IS AN OCCASION SPEECH AND WHAT SHOULD I DO?

There are many reasons for speeches. Information speeches given at conferences or meetings or to report on a company's situation or financial results, for example. Effect speeches, trying to sell ideas and persuade people, reach agreement, communicate proposals or get a consensus to carry out decisions. And, of course, there are the so-called occasion speeches, which have their place in your private as well as your business life.

What is an occasion speech? An occasion speech can open and conclude an event. For example, it can welcome people, introduce other speakers and thank them at the end. It can be an after-dinner speech, one given at a celebration (to honour long-serving or retiring employees, for example); or at an office party or to congratulate apprentices on passing their exams. Occasion speeches are given to *celebrate*, *entertain* or to just *create an atmosphere* to introduce or conclude a meeting. Here is an important tip to begin with.

> **Occasion speeches should not be longer than three to five minutes!**

First of all, however, let's look at a different scenario: what do you do if you don't want to speak at all? It happens quite frequently that someone is asked to give a speech out of the blue. Has that ever happened to you? If it has, it will have brought home to you how hard it can be to speak when you are unprepared. It can happen to anyone – and, sooner or later, it will certainly happen to you if it has not done so already.

However, there are a few tricks that can save the situation – and yourself. Prepare yourself for an 'unprepared' speech.

A scenario

During a meal, the host suddenly asks you 'to say a few words'. First of all, play hard to get! Point out that surely there are many more competent people present who could do the job far better than you. Maybe they'll take you at your word. If not, you will at least gain some time. You can gain even more time if you have a suitable excuse up your sleeve. For example, ask whether you can just go and wash your hands first or suggest postponing the speech until a better moment – say after the meal or during coffee. That way you can use the time to quickly put together a short draft. Think briefly about how to begin, write down some key words for the main structure and formulate two or three good sentences to finish with. The key words are the thread you can use to guide you through your speech and to 'hang on to'. Notes – even brief ones – provide some security and support.

Then, when you are standing there and feel the participants' expectant eyes on you, ask yourself the six W-questions: '*Who* is here?', '*Where* are we?', '*Why* are we here?', '*What* are we doing here?', '*What* would people like to hear?', '*When* should I start – and stop?' Put the questions to yourself in your mind and give the answers to them aloud, as pillars for your speech. In between, you can build in additional ideas. After all, you have some time now (as well as during your speech) to give it some thought.

If you can't think of anything suitable quickly, pick an idea at random – a current news item, for example. This could be the share index, the oil price, a newspaper clip, something that has happened that day, an anniversary or a sports event. All you need to do then is build an imaginary bridge to your participants.

Another emergency solution is 'to go into neutral' or freewheel. Just get going, speak, mention an interesting subject, nice people, the time is too short, special occasion, good food, pleasant atmosphere, stimulating conversation, successful evening – there's enough there to build on.

The best trick of all for making sure you don't fall flat on your face with an unprepared speech is to prepare one. When in doubt *always* be prepared for a speech and then nothing can go wrong! To be invited as a special guest to a club and not to prepare is foolish! To take an historical example of what to do we have only to look at Winston Churchill. He was once suddenly asked at a dinner to give a short political speech. He gave such an impressive one that everyone present was thrilled. Churchill explained freely that it was no wonder the speech went well – he had rewritten it five times and rehearsed it another three in front of a mirror! So, be prepared! If you are ever asked to give a short after-dinner speech, you stand a good chance of shining if you have an 'unprepared', prepared speech.

And if all of that will not do? Then, refuse to speak. They will find someone else who will volunteer to risk their own skin.

In order to tailor your communication to the event, you should classify occasion speeches as being entertainment, celebration or bracket speeches.

ENTERTAINMENT SPEECHES

Occasions Social gatherings (office parties, social events, outings, etc.).

Aim To create a good atmosphere among the participants.

Techniques

- Be natural. Don't be too stiff and business-like. Use simple, relaxed everyday language, as if you were having a chat.

- Don't talk about work subjects and don't try to abuse the occasion and, say, give an information speech.

- Make it no longer than five minutes.

- The occasion is a jovial one and so should you be. You are supposed to be the entertainer here. If you are good at being humorous, make a humorous speech! Entertain the participants as best you can.

- When telling stories, funny episodes or anecdotes, use the word 'Imagine ...' as the introduction. This is a good test, too. If no one can imagine the situation from what you are saying, your ability to communicate is not up to scratch. Revamp it or leave it out if that happens. Let it be followed by '... you feel', '... you are confronted', '... you want' and so on – not 'I'. Creep into people's skins, don't oblige them to creep into yours. Be entirely yourself during an entertainment speech and leave your title, your social standing and any airs and graces at the door. Show a friendly face, in keeping with the event: those who smile, win!

- Try to involve all the participants as social gatherings should not exclude anyone (this is important, especially when you know there are some sensitive people present, who are easily prone to feeling neglected).

- When giving after-dinner speeches abroad, take into account the attitude of the country in question towards your country and nationality. For example, if you come from a country where the people are viewed by others as being arrogant, be modest in your behaviour and in what you say. Make an effort to try and show your hosts that you know what goes down well in their country, what is important, popular subjects and what they enjoy. To do this, you should familiarize yourself in advance with the guest country's culture and customs. Current events or things that have just happened of course have a particularly good effect, provided they really can be translated into an anecdote that strikes a chord. So do use appropriate quotations from famous personalities of the guest country. And, say at least one sentence in the country's language. This has a tremendous impact. Remember John F. Kennedy during his visit to Germany saying, 'Ich bin ein Berliner' (I am a Berliner). As a conclusion, make a toast to your hosts and ask everyone to raise their glasses.

Tactical tips Remember to be different. Be original! Look for an unusual opening. Relax the atmosphere. Never use chronological lists or lengthy narrations in an entertaining speech. That will bore everyone to tears. Props and AP of course. Some useful props in this context are, for example, a glass, menu, bottle of wine, fax, certificate, photo, picture, watch, pen, compass and so on, or a symbolic object, such as a globe, stopwatch, stirrup, share certificate.

CELEBRATION SPEECHES

Occasions Special events (anniversaries, retirement parties, jubilees, weddings, birthdays, etc.)

Aim Appreciation.

Techniques At no time do people lie more than before an election, after a hunt and during wars. Anniversaries and funerals also come pretty close. Therefore, be particularly careful as there is only a very fine line between warmth of expression and overdramatic phrases. Try to involve everyone present. Use 'we' constantly in your speech and get rid of any trace of egocentricity. That includes self-centred memories as well, such as 'I still recall …'. Use joint experiences instead. Don't overload your celebration speech – remember that the participants want to celebrate, not listen reverently. Therefore, shorten the content of your speech!

Tactical tips There are a few special rules for work anniversaries, retirement celebrations, new appointments and staff leaving parties. You should, for example, direct the setting yourself – or at least influence it. That includes the selection of people present, choice of venue and decisions concerning other organizational issues.

Find out, well in advance, all you can about the person(s) who is being celebrated to give your speech real content. Who better to ask than their long-standing colleagues and friends? They will be able to tell you stories and anecdotes from the life of the retiring person or the person celebrating an anniversary. If you find that there is nothing about their professional lives, try to find out something about their leisure activities, hobbies, etc. Who knows, you might find that one of your employees who was thought to be rather boring in the office has pursued a really fascinating hobby or is an expert in an unusual field. Every person has a remarkable talent somewhere or likes to do something out of the ordinary. You might also talk to the honoured person themselves beforehand and find out what they want to hear. Under no circumstances should you just look up their file and chronicle their professional career: 'joined the firm 1 October 1956 as a trainee, passed the exams 10 April 1959, was given power of attorney 30 May 1965 …'. If you can't find anything at all, before the event, ask a colleague or the line manager of the person in question before the event to tell a few anecdotes about the person. The individual's own particular achievements are far more interesting than the fact that they have never called in sick in the 20 years they have been working for the firm. For example, 'Can you remember when Site 2 caught fire in 1985? It was you, Charlie, who was the first to run over to the shed and come back dragging the hosepipe along'.

We all know from experience that it is often very hard for older colleagues to leave 'their' company. To make it easier for them, avoid using phrases like 'the rest of your life'. It would be better to say something like, 'The second part of your life is now about to begin'. The tenor of your speech should be, 'We envy you'. You can say it, too: 'Next time we sit in yet another traffic jam on our way to work, you'll be sitting at home, enjoying a leisurely breakfast'. They should, in any case, be encouraged to break away from the company – maybe start some studies or be given a special project.

There are various props you could use – an old photo, certificates of achievement, medals, newspaper cuttings, objects they have made, letters, etc. You might, say, ask the others present to pick out the person in an old group photograph: 'Do you recognize him?' Hand the company's gift over only at the end of your speech (for a retiring person this could be a holiday, for example). And, in addition, as a memory of the day, why not give them a video of the manager's speech, which can be proudly watched again and again.

Special rules for office parties

A party is a party and you should not use the occasion to talk about work-related subjects or give an overview of the past year. Nor should you make critical remarks about work productivity or absenteeism. Such subjects are out of place at a party. Don't turn a cheerful office party into a stiff banquet either – unless you want your staff to feel ill at ease. The atmosphere at a company party should be relaxed (small tables, mixed seating order). A party that is announced as a banquet easily ends up being a demonstration of status. Let a staff committee take over responsibility for organizing the event. They often have a better feel for what their colleagues hope for and expect of such an event than their bosses. So, the party committee, consisting of members of staff, works out the programme for the event, determines the seating order and schedule and possibly makes necessary transport arrangements. What about the entertainment? The best option would be to have your own staff provide it. Use inside talent. You achieve AP that way. It also lets you off the hook: all you, as the boss, need to do is give a short speech at the end, thanking everyone!

Special rules for inaugurations, openings

These occasions are ideal opportunities for positive PR. For example, if you have to give a speech at the opening of a new factory your company has built or bought, you should use this to enhance your firm's relationships with the general public, other neighbouring firms, local politicians and authorities, as well as with your employees and their families.

Choose the right arguments here: fewer success facts and figures and material ambitions and more about social benefits and motivational topics instead. This is a rare opportunity to build a solid feeling of trust and positive reactions. Only emphasize common objectives that reinforce the feeling of belonging together. After your speech, local people, municipal representatives and your staff must have the feeling that the new factory is 'their' factory.

Assume personal overall control of your speech and delegate details – otherwise, you will be faced with unforeseen problems that can confuse you and cause you to fail. Make sure the event is being properly organized, that there is some spare time, that the seating order is right and the guests have been identified. Make people feel at ease and strike a warm, friendly (not pompous) note.

Try to get out of having to mention every single guest of honour during your welcoming speech. Only mention the most important guest of honour ('Your Honour...') and the others jointly ('... With you, we extend a warm welcome to all our guests of honour').

During your speech, speak in a natural tone, don't dramatize and keep things in proportion! Your new, fully-automated production line is *not* the ninth wonder of the world!

On the other hand, if you are invited to an opening or inauguration as a guest of a company or their subsidiary with whom you have good relations, you can enhance your own relationships with those around you at such events, too. Give a well-prepared speech and try to be the first to speak – no one can pre-empt what you are going to say, then, and you don't have to struggle with the aftermath of any lengthy and boring earlier speeches. Don't be too modest or timid – you can easily mention the name of your own company three or four times during your speech.

Overall control is again important here. Gather material for your speech by directly questioning people beforehand (hardly any of the other speakers will do that). Find out what other speakers are going to say. Have a say in where you are going to stand and how you are going to be announced to the audience. Check the equipment to be used in good time! Double-check the sequence of events just before your appearance as, perhaps, there have been some last-minute changes. And, by all means let the previous speaker or the organizer hand you the microphone, but don't refer to them. If they were good, the participants will be pleasantly reminded of them (instead of listening to you). If they were bad, the audience will fear the same of you. Don't forget: express genuine warmth, solidarity and appreciation.

BRACKET (SCENE-SETTING SPEECHES)

Occasions Opening and closing events introducing and thanking main or guest speakers.

Aim To create a positive platform (before and after) for the event.

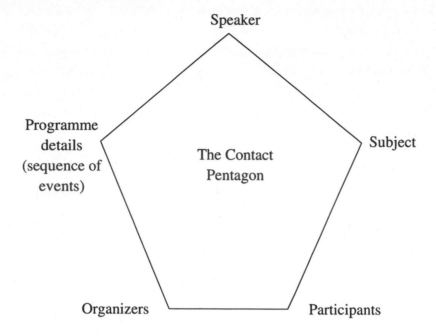

Techniques Create a 'contact pentagon'. To do this, bear the following five points in mind when drawing up your opening or introductory speech and your expression of thanks and closing remarks for the event.

- speaker/communicator
- subject
- participants
- organizers
- programme details.

You want to give the event a good start and a good ending with your introductory and concluding remarks. This also means that you are not the most important person. This limits your task. At the beginning you could open by saying, '*Why* this speaker, this subject, *why* these participants, this organizer, this programme?' Ask these five questions to start with. You will put the participants in a positive frame of mind and arouse their curiosity about what is to follow. That is your content.

After the presentation or event, you say a few words of thanks, to round off the occasion. At that point, you *answer* these very five questions: 'That is why ...'

So, you start out with (rhetorical) questions and you conclude by proving your opening points, like brackets containing the whole. In this way, you create a communicative frame or setting around the presentation given by the main speaker. For example, regarding the subject you could begin with, 'Why are we all gathered here today to discuss this subject?', and end with, 'And this is why we have gathered here today to discuss this subject'.

Of course, you won't start your introductory or concluding speech with worn-out phrases such as, 'Ladies and gentlemen. I have the honourable task of ...'. The following is much better: 'You, too, probably sometimes have the urge to leave it all behind. Too much stress, too many battles, too many trivialities, too many strains. With us here tonight is a man who, until recently, shared the same view – but even more keenly. His name is Tony Sharp, and Tony, you are now going to tell us why you ...'

Let us now look at the five sides of the contact pentagon in greater detail.

1 The speaker is the most important person at the event. For this reason, coordinate or agree on your introduction with them beforehand. When you then introduce them, don't say: 'Dr Jenny Wright has ...', but 'You, Dr Wright, have ...'. You, as the bracket (scene-setting) speaker, are standing in their shadow; you create the platform for them. When you introduce the speaker to the participants, it is important to sell them properly. Many masters of ceremony (MCs) – if they don't commit the even bigger sin of putting themselves on centre stage – make the mistake of praising the main speaker to the roof and, thus, creating expectations on the part of the participants that are almost impossible to fulfil. You'll be digging the speaker's own grave if you oversell them. Only if you know that the expectations of the participants are negative do you have to try and reverse these attitudes or prejudices, improve the atmosphere and create a more positive curiosity. You can do this, for example, by painting a positive character image of the speaker. This, however, should be limited to traits that are relevant to the event in question. For example, if you want to sell a NATO General to a group of environmentalists, you could point out that the General actively supports the environmental group in his native town, that one of his sons is a member of Greenpeace and that biology is his hobby. His brilliant military career and his family's long tradition of producing high-ranking officers is something you should probably not mention in this context.

2 **The subject** When you touch on the subject in your introduction speech, the main purpose should be to arouse interest, make the participants curious. That means you only *hint* at the news to come or the extraordinary knowledge of the speaker. Use rhetorical questions – positive statements in the form of a question. Never pre-empt what the main speaker is going to say, and never steal their thunder. Bracket speakers eager to puff up their own egos just destroy the atmosphere.

3 **The participants** Greet them in a way that motivates them and keeps them receptive. You are already aware of EMMA as a way to start. Give the participants guidance on how to react during the main speech (with questions, contributions to the discussion, interrupting the speaker, taking notes, getting actively involved, etc.). But, only after prior consultation with, and the agreement of, the main speaker. One important aspect of the first contact between participants and speaker is often overlooked: introduce the participants to the speaker as well. 'Malcolm Crow and Andrew Berry are members of the local mountain rescue team. The lady behind them is Dr Caroline Bingley, Consultant at the hospital here. She is accompanied by two of her nurses, Jackie Brown and Fiona Smith. Finally, to the left of Malcolm, is Trevor Bower from St Johns' Ambulance'. Also, it is important to only mention the people present. Ignore 'absent friends' – those guests or participants who failed to show up. You demotivate both the speaker and the participants by mentioning everyone who was invited but did not come, for whatever reason. Also forget their more or less well-meaning

messages, be they apologies, support of the cause, recommendations and expressions of regret for being absent.

4 The organizers When should you say something about the organizers of the event in your opening and closing address? When they are not generally known or if the initiator of the event is to be emphasized for PR reasons or when you want to create some positive advertising. For example, 'The reason we, of all people, have invited you to this event today is a very special one ...'. Beware, though, due to egocentric motives, this part often becomes too long, so remember KISS.

5 The programme details It is part of your responsibilities to inform the participants about the programme or the order of events before the start, give them an overview of the agenda, the timing, organizational details, breaks, contact opportunities and, possibly, guidelines about the general conduct. By the way, which point should you begin with? That is entirely up to you, but, when in doubt, always check with the main speaker first. Start with the participants themselves, unless there are good reasons not to.

And how do you communicate unpleasant changes to the participants? Don't worry, it's not that difficult. Here are some examples.

- You have to replace the speaker. Phrase it positively: 'Instead of Joe S, who unfortunately can't make it here today, we have the pleasure of welcoming you, Jim B, here among us. Of course, from your past experience you know the set-up here better than anyone else from outside'. The substitute speaker should appear like a gift sent from heaven to the participants.
- The speaker is not or not well enough prepared. Don't draw the participants' attention to this fact, keep the knowledge of it to yourself. Otherwise, the participants will hang on every word the speaker utters, hoping to spot mistakes and gaps in the presentation. Frequently, the participants won't even notice the problem. If they do so, however, you can always say a few conciliatory words at the end.

- Your speaker has to cancel at the very last minute. That is bad indeed. Yet, there are still two possibilities open to you: either you take over the part of the main speaker as well or you organize a general discussion on the subject in question.
- Your speaker is late. Unfortunately this happens quite often. This is your chance to prove your talent for improvization and entertain the participants or you could simply bring forward a break that was planned for later or another programme item.
- Your speaker is unwell. In this case the same applies as in the second example above: don't draw the participants' attention to the fact. Mentioning this will not serve to protect the speaker – on the contrary, it will only make the participants keen to spot weaknesses in their presentation. You can achieve a completely different effect if you admit to the participants after the speech that the speaker was actually unwell. This is bound to trigger double applause.

You see, there are very few hopeless situations. By the way, don't finish with the pompous phrase, 'And now I hand you over to Joe S'. Better to say, 'Joe, we are curious about ...'. At the end of the event, after the main speaker's presentation, again say a few words. The fact that you are going to do that, however, has to be communicated to the participants during your introduction and before the main speech, otherwise they will get up after applauding the main speaker and leave the room. Your conclusion has to be quick, short and powerful. If not, the participants will leave even as you speak. Long explanations, repetitions or additional, complicated thoughts have no place here as the participants have heard it all in the main speech already. Thanking the speaker can be integrated into your conclusion by recapping on statements made in your introduction: 'Thank you very much for your precise answers to our difficult questions about ...'. If you want to give the participants a summary of the main speech, then do it very briefly, in a short synopsis of one or two sentences. Here you can also point out the practical applications of what has been said and remind the participants of two or three of the speaker's quotes. What you should definitely avoid are meaningless, general phrases and pompous exclamations, such as, 'This impressive speech has proven once again that our economy is alive and well. It will face the challenges of tomorrow... May each and everyone of us be aware of the responsibility ...'. What you can do, however, is to offer a vision beyond the bounds of the presentation: 'Whether or not these political ideas can be put into reality in the Europe of the nineties and beyond, who knows? Opinions are divided on this point. The optimists – and that includes you and us – share the view that ...'

This gives you a few ideas on how to conclude a successful speech. What do you do, however, if the speaker's presentation was a failure? There are solutions at hand for this as well. If there are at least some positive aspects of the speech (and there are almost always *some*) you should point these out and continue the thread – thin as it may have been – and expand on or emphasize it: 'As you rightly pointed out repeatedly ..., which was very necessary. What might have sounded as if it were obvious is, in fact, very important ...', 'In this context, over the last few weeks we have ...'. Lift it up. Do everything you can to find a positive ending. It can be done, with a bit of courage and goodwill. Occasion speeches gain life more from the way in which they are pre-

> **Now you can no doubt answer the four questions and solve the four problems.**

sented than from their content. Emphasize your tone of voice, show genuine warmth and express feelings. Use episodes, quotes and examples. Appeal to emotions. Create an atmosphere. And remember EMMA and KISS!

2. Information speeches

Can you answer the following four questions?

1 **What comes first: informing or motivating?**

2 **Why are most information speeches rather boring?**

3 **How many facts, figures and details can you pack into an information speech?**

4 **Can you put questions to the participants in an information speech to involve them? If yes, what kinds of questions?**

Can you solve the following four problems?

1 Robert Elliott, owner of a medium-sized company producing parts for the automotive industry, gives a longish, impressive speech about the company's plans for the coming year at the Christmas party. He describes the firm's objectives, the competition, market conditions and then appeals to all members of staff to do their duty and give their best to ensure that these objectives are met. Robert believes that he has motivated his staff with this speech.

Do you believe that too? If not, what has he not taken into account at all in his speech?

_____

_____

_____

2 Steve White, a departmental manager, is annoyed. His staff have not achieved the annual target. As their boss, he intends to tell them off, one by one. He quotes them last year's bad figures, accuses them of underperforming and talks about the consequences: 'You will see for yourselves what happens if you don't improve your performance this year. We shouldn't delude ourselves. If we have to make you redundant we're all on the scrapheap'. After a whole series of further negative statements, he concludes his speech with a range of precise, plausible recommendations, then offers a few conciliatory friendly words and finally wishes them good luck.

How would you have given this information speech? Is it not possible to call a spade a spade?

_____

_____

_____

_____

_____

3 'I consider a strong union representation in companies to be very important. A trade union needs a base in every organization to be able to achieve its aims. Only if I, as a trade unionist, know what's going on out there, will I be able to react properly. An old hand like myself, having been a union member for 20 years, believes in the strength of the trade union movement. History can quote you many examples of this. The past has proven that a great idea needs the backing of a lot of members. Especially young ones like you. Make your contribution too.' This is the introduction used by a trade unionist to inform young trainees about the task of union committees in organizations.

Do you think he will be successful with this? What should he bear in mind above all before he starts to speak?

---

4 Neil Keagan, the Managing Director of a computer firm, has been asked to introduce a computer system to several senior managers of a medium-sized import-export trading house, who had been recommended to purchase the system. He has prepared his presentation very well and, after a brief welcome, leaps straight into the subject: 'The operating system Unix ensures total compatibility with and full integrability of all different kinds of hardware from all leading specialist providers of networked workstations and servers.' As Neil is about to explain how the system works in more detail, he is interrupted by one of the managers: 'I am sorry, but I haven't understood a word you've said. Besides, what use is it to me?'

Neil has made a big mistake. What is it?

THE FIVE REQUIREMENTS AND SOME USEFUL TIPS

Information is about filling gaps in someone's knowledge. The aim of information speeches is to improve the participants' knowledge, put them in the picture and explain contexts. To achieve that you have to satisfy requirement No. 1: to *motivate*. Every listener asks the question: 'What's in it for me?' If you can't answer this question satisfactorily right at the outset, your speech will be a waste of time. How many information speeches truly fulfil this elementary requirement.

When engineer Tony White explains to the client company's technicians how a certain machine is constructed, then this is an information speech. When he goes one step further and explains to them how the machine has to be operated as well – and familiarizes the participants with the process, then it turns into an instruction speech. Instruction speeches also fall into the category of information speeches. And they, too, have to motivate.

What are the occasions for information speeches? They include internal subjects relating to the company as well as external ones, ranging from employee briefings at work to reports on the accounts of a sports club. An information speech has to be clearly structured. Otherwise it does not fulfil requirement No. 2: to be *easily understood*! You have to take the participants through the subject one step at a time. That's why careful preparation is the key to success.

Your aim is to inform. That also means to influence. You can use all the communication methods you have learnt from the previous chapters and apply them with even more intensity, as the subject matter is usually dry and sober.

This brings us to requirement No. 3: *activate* the participants and *make* constant *use of audio-visual aids.* Pictures, slides and transparencies make complicated processes, technical details and even large quantities of data come alive. Constantly remind the participants of the practical use they can make of them ('this will enable you to ...') and do so after every point you make.

The participants must feel that you have tailored the content specifically to them. So, *empathize*. That is requirement No. 4. 'You' is your core word. Your 'I' will interest the participants not a jot. Try to supply some graphic illustrations to add to the bare facts. This also reduces the risk of each of them creating their own interpretations and reaching their own conclusions.

Give a summary at the latest every five minutes. Every 10 to 15 minutes, introduce a break: 'OK, a short break. What have you noted down so far? There are three important points here ...'. You may also underline these short interim summaries by distributing handouts. *Breaks and interim summaries* are requirement No. 5.

The prepared written summary of the first part also makes the participants ready to take in a further chunk of information. 'What are the conclusions to be drawn from these various figures, ladies and gentlemen?' *Checking understanding* is requirement No. 6.

A further tip: give another summary of the whole at the end! And, again, emphasize the practical use the participants can make of the information provided. A few further tactical tips: constantly help the participants to keep up with your input! Tell them time and again where exactly in your presentation you are. Tell them as you proceed: 'That is enough on writers in general. Now we'll move on to three different types of writers: fiction writers, non-fiction writers and professional writers. Please refer to page five here'. The participants have to be aware of the structure of your presentation for them to be able to place all the information you are providing where it belongs. You can captivate the participants by making them curious. How?

Promise them answers to their questions – for example, 'In five minutes at the latest you will know the answer – and you will be surprised', or, 'Which results do you think we have achieved here? At best? In the worst case?' The best participants are those that contribute actively. To facilitate this you can, for example, distribute one or two diagrams without any further explanation or description. The participants will look at you with big eyes, full of expectation. 'Put down the probable plus and minus deviations you think we will have to reckon with.' Apart from this you say nothing. Later in your presentation you come back to it: 'This shows interest rate developments and our export figures over the past few years. How much the two are related is shown by the diagram(s) in front of you. Take another look at the two curves now. Do you see? The upper curve shows the plus and the lower curve the minus deviations. And what does your own prediction look like?'

Another way of raising your participants' attention is not to reveal all the information on an overhead transparency at once. Only reveal one new point at a time. For example, a technical manager wants to get across ten important points about successful sales negotiations to her team. At first, though, she only shows the first point, explains it, gives examples and answers questions. Only then does she uncover the second point on the transparency, then the third one, etc. This keeps participants attentive and creates curiosity as to what has not yet been revealed.

Always remember that information speeches have to be explicit. One illustration says more than a thousand words. Don't use explanations that have been written by others. Digest the facts and present them in a way that a layperson can understand as well. Even when you speak in front of alleged experts don't use experts' double Dutch. It gives the impression that you have erected a façade to hide behind for fear of making a clear stand and voicing your personal opinions – if not a lack of technical knowledge and understanding.

Constantly observe the climate: a good atmosphere increases the participants' receptiveness; a bad atmosphere can destroy it. Only when your communication is powerful will the participants enjoy your information speech. Try it! You can even try completely new ways. Many of the unwritten laws of traditional, dry, informative presentations used in numerous organizations create nothing but boredom and should be thrown out, never to be used again. Anything that truly serves your aim of creating real understanding is allowed.

Another important recommendation to end with. Keep *facts* and *opinions* separate. There is a saying in journalism that goes, 'The facts of the news are sacred, the comments are free'. Take this to heart. Facts are neutral, but your personal opinion is subjective. Both can be important, but you have to draw a dividing line between them to remain credible.

TIPS FOR MEETINGS AT WORK

Information speeches are most often needed for meetings at work. Absorb the following 12 steps and meetings with your colleagues won't cause you any more communication problems. You will be able to deal with them confidently and successfully and win over and persuade people by using the right kind of approach.

1 A captivating (motivating) opening

You know the importance of this by now: no empty phrases at the beginning, but, instead, a loud bang. 'We will all be out on the street next year – if we don't act promptly', or, more positively: 'You can earn at least £4000 more per year – if you apply the following ...'

2 Provide an overview of the objective, content and roles of the participants (include this in the invitation as well)

'This is about a new strategy for our domestic market. First of all, we need to talk about the product, then about our distribution network and, finally, about the necessary marketing measures. During the next 15 minutes, we will discuss together the current position and please *do* bombard me with questions if any points are unclear. Jenny is going to take notes for us. At two o'clock we will take a break.' Put these points briefly into your agenda, sent out before the event.

3 Announcing results (short, with a value judgement)

'Our position is bad in almost all areas except one. Our market share in our most important region has dropped by 10 per cent. The market is stagnating and our competitors are catching up. But, there is some hope?'

4 The current situation (general, with a value judgement)

'The latest order figures have, again, confirmed the negative trend. If this continues, we will, at best, be beaten into second place in six months' time. This development has been a real blow for me – and I'm sure to many of you. We have to change that.'

5 Giving explanations, comments, possibly an overview (of points 3 and 4)

'The downward trend is caused by some unfortunate product policy decisions and a continually deteriorating service. This has been revealed by the analysis carried out by the management consultancy we appointed. We have already taken the first steps to making the necessary changes in our Production Department and our main emphasis is now on the service aspect and our distributors. Four years ago, we were one of many suppliers. Do you remember? Two years later, we were the number one and now our market position is, all of a sudden, crumbling again.'

6 Praising ('you') or criticizing ('we')

This is the point at which you should motivate your people. Show empathy. When you make negative comments, include yourself – it will make them easier to swallow. Recognition, though, is directed at others: '*You* have done an excellent job over the last few years. Even the competition has had to recognize that. In spite of this, *we* have made mistakes. *We* all should have noticed much earlier that...'. Just swap the words 'you' and 'we' in your mind. Can you see the difference?

7.1 Discussing a vision of the future, objectives for the next period

Now comes the link from the past to the future – the 'is' to 'should be' passage. So far, you have reminded the participants of the situation in the past and the current state of affairs. The important thing now is to describe what is supposed to happen from this moment on. Put it that way too, for example, 'All of that belongs to the past. We now have to look ahead. There is a lot to be done to get us out of our dilemma. But one step at a time. Our next objective is that, until the end of the quarter we'll have to ...'.

7.2 Discussing ways and means of achieving the objective (possibly in the form of a dialogue)

In order to motivate the participants, you have to involve them. This is best done in the form of a conversation – with AP. Try it this way, for example, 'How can we achieve our objective? What do you think?' Or you could address one colleague directly: 'There are several ways to get there. Tony, when we were talking last week, you made an interesting suggestion. Could you repeat it here please?', followed by, 'Then we will have a joint brainstorming session for additional solutions'. If you manage to work out jointly the ways and means of achieving the objective, the participants will, in all probability, also be committed to them and actively participate in putting them into action.

7.3 Gaining agreement

This is the prime requirement. Without the participants' agreement, you have little chance of the measures actually coming about. You can achieve the desired consent by painting the objective in a positive light, offering benefits and promises and phrasing your questions in such a way that the participants only have to respond with 'Yes': 'Do we want to choose this way? Will we achieve it? So that we will all earn more, increase our job satisfaction and improve together? Do we want to try it? You, too? Immediately? If so, we have achieved a lot today'.

8 Checking that it is all agreed

If you are still unsure as to whether or not the participants really *are* completely behind you, ask again or let them vote on it. An important tip: write down what decision has been taken. Send an action plan to every participant, otherwise you may have to start from scratch again next time.

9 General projects and future goals; offer visions

Convey a broad, positive perspective to the participants that goes beyond the achievement of the objective of that meeting presenting a total picture to them: 'In two years at the latest, we will be at the top again. Then we can embark on our next expansion phase, the creation of branches all over the world. Who knows which of you will then have the opportunity to work in Canada or Brazil. But, in the meantime, you will be interested to hear that the Board has had very promising negotiations ...'.

10 Participants' questions

If you want to encourage the participants to ask questions, you can do so by saying simply, 'Any questions?' , or, 'Is there anything else you would like to know about this?' If one or other of the participants at the meeting has still got any reservations, you can eliminate them here. At any rate, the participants have another chance to say something before you close the meeting. That way no one feels bulldozed.

11 Give three tips for improving performance

Do you remember the magic figure three? Anyone can remember three tips. So, give your people three good pieces of advice to take away: 'Do you know how our boss prepares over the weekend for the week ahead? He does three things which you may want to try, too:

- first, he has a look at the increasing share prices of our competitors and gets very annoyed about it
- second, he goes for a half-hour run, then for an hour's swim and switches off completely
- third, he prepares himself mentally to personally win one more order in the coming week than he did last week.

We can all do that as well, can't we?'

Running a meeting without giving any well-planned tips on how participants can improve their performance in the future is to waste a valuable, unique opportunity. You cannot change the past. What you can do, however, is offer a vision of the future.

12 The conclusion, conveying a feeling of achievement, making the goal appealing (using empathy)

The conclusion has to be powerful. The last few sentences have to signal your determination, and motivate the participants: 'We are a great team. If we continue to stick together and we all keep this goal in mind, then no competitor can stop us. Thanks to your help, we have today managed to lay the foundation, achieving a great deal already, don't you think?'

These 12 steps will help you deliver a successful information speech at work meetings.

TIPS FOR COMMENTS ON ANNUAL CORPORATE FINANCIAL PERFORMANCE

As a senior manager, you will have to comment on annual reports. There is ample scope for mistakes here! But, you don't have to make them. The following are a few ideas for how to do it right.

Aim

Determine in advance for yourself what you want to achieve with your analysis. Put it into just one sentence that is well thought out, using precise and accurate phrases. For example, 'The fall in our profitability caused by our tremendous expansion has to be corrected this year'.

Structure

Look at each of the points you want to make and the way you want to present them and ask yourself: 'Does it serve the purpose I have set myself?' For example, you are talking about your firm's strong growth and wonder whether or not to mention the fact that your exports to Canada have fallen by 10 per cent, whereas the profits in percentage terms have reduced only slightly. No, this does not serve your purpose. And the strike in France? This is not relevant to this context either. The following points provide an excellent structure for a speech at such an occasion.

The assignment

1 Looking back and assessing past performance

Communicate your value criteria. Don't quote any figures yet, but show trends and developments. For example, 'The economy has again hardly grown in the past year, thus continuing the trend of the previous few years. The whole economy is lacking the stimulating elements from abroad that influenced the situation at the end of the 1980s. This can be attributed to the relationship between our currency and the US dollar, which has made our export trade increasingly difficult. We have, however, been successful thanks to our diversification policy, but our increased turnover has also caused higher costs'.

2 Results and achievements

This is where the figures have their place. Present them so that they are easy to understand. Use visual aids, such as slides, drawings, graphs or diagrams. For example, 'We have grown by 20 per cent in the last year. Our turnover increased from £80 to £396 million and the number of staff employed from 200 to 240. Turnover has not grown at the same rate in all areas. For example, the compact disc sector shows a growth rate of 25 per cent, whereas cassette sales increased by 12 per cent, and albums by 8 per cent. You can see these welcome growth figures in the curves on the graph. We are thus performing well above the industry average in all three sectors, as is illustrated by this diagram. As far as CDs are concerned, our increase was 5 per cent higher than the competition average. With cassettes, we are 2 per cent above the industry average and, again, 2 per cent up for albums'. These are sound pieces of data, but, unless you illustrate them, people will still have problems taking them in.

3 Interpreting results and achievements

Now comes the proof of the figures. How did you achieve these results and performances? You could, for example, say 'What are the reasons for our success? We placed our bets on the CD market earlier than our competitors. In the spring we had already launched a special advertising campaign for this new product and nearly doubled the display space for CDs. We have also increased our selection of music cassettes and restricted ourselves to two main areas for vinyl: LPs and classical music'.

4 The current position

Now you describe what the situation is today. What has happened since the report was finalized? What is going to happen now? Caution! Use 'Provided that ...' so you don't get caught out. Let's use the example from the music industry again to illustrate this: 'The trend towards CDs has continued in the first three months of this year. Sales of cassettes have also kept on growing. With albums, however, there has been a noticeable decline. Approximately 10 per cent of album buyers appear to have finally switched to CDs or cassettes only. This will cause problems for us. Our total turnover for last month is 30 per cent higher than for the same month last year. Provided that this development continues over the next few months, the current financial year will be a record. My estimate is that we will achieve a growth of 30 per cent in our turnover by the end of the year. This, however, will be offset by increased costs that we will have to absorb.'

5 Prospects and objectives for the future

To turn to our example once more, 'For the late 1990s and beyond, we are expecting another change in buyer behaviour. The CD will establish itself as the most important sound media, whereas the LP will slowly but surely almost disappear. There will be a small number of customers who will continue to buy them. Serving them will cost money and use up funds, which we only have to a limited extent. Of course, we will have to keep as broad a spectrum of products on sale as possible over the years to come, but not at any cost. If we forecast the trend incorrectly, we will be out of the game in five years' time. On the other hand, if we manage to match customers' demands and tastes fully, we will soon reach the number one position. In five years' time we will then have a turnover of £200 million pounds, with a staff of around 500 and a good return on capital'.

6 Thanks and appeal for action

Thank everyone involved for their work in achieving the results you have just informed them about and appeal to the participants for their continued commitment and help in the future. Don't conclude with just an abrupt: 'Good luck'. One possible ending could be, 'Let me thank all of you here at head office, our colleagues in the branch offices and our sales force for their commitment over the past year. Without your contribution we would not have been able to present these results today. We should all continue like this in the year to come. Then, we will together achieve our objective of increasing turnover and reducing costs by the end of the year! This will allow us to award at least normal salary increases; with your help hopefully we will be able to have more than that.' Don't forget that your intention is to *make a comment* on the annual report, that is, explain the most important points, not to repeat the whole report in your own words. So, keep it much shorter than you may have intended. Remember too, that your overall goal is commitment for future results. Focus on this.

HOW TO GIVE AN ACCOUNT OF A SPECIAL PROJECT

Special projects or tasks often require a report to be made after their completion. You are supposed to 'account for something' and that may create uneasy feelings. But, even these reports are manageable, just read the next few pages! If you follow the outlined structure, you will soon master this form of communication as well. The aim and general structure of this kind of report are very similar to those for giving a report on the annual corporate financial performance. Both cover the outcome of a particular period of time.

Aim

Determine for yourself what you want to achieve with this report. Describe it in just one well thought out sentence, precisely and clearly phrased. For example, you have received the assignment, to find out which topics your management magazine should focus on in order that its intended market – senior managerial people – will buy it at an up-market price. You want to say in your report that 'If our new magazine offers managers decision-making tools in a concise form, only then will it stand a chance of being successfully positioned at a higher price bracket'.

Structure

Using the structure set out below and for each of the points and in the way you present them, ask yourself whether or not they will serve the purpose you have set yourself.

1 Define the task

What was the nature of your assignment? What were you supposed to find out? Using our publishing example, you could say 'We want to create a new, top-level management magazine. My assignment was to determine which subjects to focus on in order to introduce it success-fully with a sufficiently big circulation at the higher end of the price range'. Here you ask for agreement from your participants that this was indeed the assignment as it could be that you interpreted it too widely or too narrowly.

2 Starting point

What was the position when you took on the project? This point should only be mentioned if appropriate. For example: 'The situation was that there had been no market research nor any definite knowledge gained from experience. I therefore had to start from zero. The given time scale was six weeks.'

3.1 Result

What have you achieved through your work? Don't explain your procedure at this point, nor describe your results chronologically. Rather, present your conclusion: 'Our research has shown that the market segment we want to target is already overloaded with information publications. These are felt to be too basic, general and dispensable. None of them are very successful and not a single magazine has managed to position itself in the upper price bracket. If ours really offers the decision-making tools we promise, then it has a chance – but no more. Price, then, is almost irrelevant.'

3.2 Expanding on the points

You could possibly go into how you have arrived at your results and, if required, what methods you have used at this stage in your report. You should again determine how much time to give this point by considering how closely it relates to your objective. Maybe the participants only want to hear your overall results and are not interested in *how* you obtained them. Perhaps, though, you may want to give at least a summary of the methods you used for tactical reasons (to show that you have been thorough and that you have worked well). How you decide to approach this depends on each individual case. If in doubt, check by using AP.

4.1 Factual conclusions

Only mention objective consequences or conclusions, those that can be checked and proven with figures.

For example, 'Our research has shown that only one in three chief executives can be targeted with our magazine. This still makes a group of approximately 40 000 potential customers. The figures prove the following. If we produce a 30- to 40-page magazine, 40 per cent of which is advertising space, at an annual subscription price of about £190, we will reach break-even point with the number of copies we expect to sell'.

4.2 Possible conclusions

This is the place for subjective conclusions, those that cannot be proven but which you feel are important and conceivable. Add your judgement and time indications, where possible. Try to avoid descriptive adjectives such as soon, later, shortly, considerable, satisfactory, welcome. Let's draw on our publishing example again for an idea of what a good possible conclusion sounds like: 'The target market for our magazine is so important that there should be no problem in getting the advertising industry interested in buying space in such a product. We could also conceivably couple the advertising with that of our three existing magazines, in which case, we can expect some synergic effects. On the basis of the results of the analysis carried out during the past few weeks, I consider that a magazine of the type described is economically viable, but only just barely profitable. We will have to calculate on there being an introductory phase of 7 to 12 months before we reach break-even point.'

5 Suggestions

You now make suggestions about the action to be taken, based on these conclusions. That will help the decision making – provided that a decision is requested (whether or not you ask for one will depend on the task you were given and your role in the company). An example of how you could ask for a decision could go like this, 'If we publish this magazine solely for commercial reasons, I recommend that we don't go ahead. On the other hand, what risks are we willing to take? And what other projects would have to wait if we went ahead with this one?'

6 Further points (observations)

Present your 'marginal' observations and mention possible consequences for other work areas. For instance, 'We have discovered
through our research and analysis that there seems to be an interesting
market for high-flyers and career people. So far, no publisher has
brought out a product to serve this segment, so we could take on a pio-
neering role here. By the way, we have noticed that the managerial
newsletters that used to be so popular are now suffering from falling
sales, with one or two exceptions'. Therefore, maybe other market seg-
ments could be targeted.

7 Summary (indispensable for any report over five minutes)

Only now do you present a brief summary of the points you've mentioned so far. For example, 'To summarize briefly, the aim of my
assignment was to find out ... . The three most important results are ...'.

8 Release from the task or new project

Ask whether or not the task you were given has now been fulfilled, or
your findings lead to a new or follow-up assignment. There must be no
remaining doubts. Is the task finished or not? Should you do more?
This is how such a report *should* be structured and presented. Unfortunately, it is far too rarely done this way. Make this structure your own.
Of course, such a report frequently becomes a dialogue with clarifying
questions, requests for explanation and so on, and then the structure
becomes even *more* important!

> You will now be able to answer the questions at
> the beginning of this chapter and solve the four
> problems described there, too.

Your information speeches must, above all, motivate. This can't be done by simply and conventionally stringing facts, figures, trends and forecasts together. As information speeches are not spectacular in their content or objective, you have to do everything possible to make their presentation exciting. Break with counter-productive, thoughtless traditions.

3. Effect speeches

Can you answer the following four questions?

1 In front of which type of participants do you give a persuasive, a motivation or an action speech?

2 What is the meaning of the 'tunnel principle' for an action speech?

3 What is your understanding of the phrase 'To win over, not to overcome'?

4 Is an action speech based primarily on emotions or on logical facts? Or on both?

Can you solve the following four problems?

1 John Martinez, Marketing Manager of a forklift truck manufacturer, gives a sales presentation to a group of senior managers from a client company, which has hinted that it might place a large order for 300 vehicles. John presents his company as a highly efficient organization, reacting flexibly to customer requirements. He shows they are capable of delivering even large quantities at a high quality within a very short space of time. All his arguments are well supported and underline the company's reliability. The longer his presentation takes, the more the participants get bored and they even show signs of being irritable. John had politely asked them to save their questions until the end of his presentation.

Why does John not manage to persuade the group?

_____

_____

_____

2 A representative of the Red Cross calls on the members of a business club to donate humanitarian aid to the victims of an earthquake in a developing country. The listeners are quite prepared to make a contribution. At the end, the speaker, who wants to avoid giving the impression of being pushy, says, 'Please give some thought to what you can do – whether you would like to donate money or provide first-aid items and how your aid can be transported to the area hit by the catastrophe. Any contributions you make will be welcome'. His intention not to press the businesspeople present was praiseworthy, but not very useful.

The speaker had a great opportunity, but he missed it. What should he have done differently?

_____

_____

_____

3 You are talking to your staff about new regional marketing measures to strengthen customer loyalty. Your staff are also convinced that this is a good idea as you had together already agreed on these measures a few weeks previously, during a sales conference. You recap again on all the arguments mentioned before, in order to persuade your staff. On top of that, you add several new points.

Instead of meeting with enthusiasm, however, you are, all of a sudden, confronted with scepticism and doubts. Somehow, you seem to have approached your staff (who before were already convinced) in the wrong way. Can you think what you have done wrong or left out?

_____

_____

_____

4 Neil Guttenberg, Director of Research and Development for a car radio manufacturer, gives a short, convincing presentation to the members of the Board about the development efforts that need to be made in order to increase the firm's product range to include car telephones. In his very lively speech, he says why the Board should agree to a research budget, mentions the difficulties that may arise, but also offers plausible solutions. He ends with the words, 'May I ask for your agreement?!' The reaction of the Board members is rather disappointing. There is silence. Instead of getting spontaneous agreement, he is told, 'We will have to think this over again thoroughly and should postpone making this important decision until the next meeting.'

Neil feels that he has met with failure. How could he have made the members of the Board decide then and there?

_____

_____

_____

_____

THE OBJECTIVE OF EFFECT SPEECHES

Of course, effect speeches contain information as well. Apart from that, however, the two are very different in their aims and approaches. Effect speeches have one simple principle as their objective – only achieving what you have set out to achieve; the fulfilment of your goal is what counts. You should also differentiate between *persuasion speeches, motivation speeches* and *action speeches*. With a persuasion speech you want to influence the participants, with a motivation you want to stimulate them and with an action speech you want to achieve a concrete action or decision.

PERSUASIVE SPEECHES

Occasions

Presentations, meetings, conferences, negotiations.

Target group's attitude

Either opponents (people who hold different opinions) or indifferent people (uninterested), ranging from negative to neutral.

Aim

To influence, convince, convert, sell, win, change attitudes.

Techniques

- Use intellectually acceptable arguments as well as emotion to win them over to your point of view.

- A lot of empathy; start from the participants' point of view. Use 'you' consistently in the opening phrase.

- Less power, especially at the beginning, to avoid giving the impression that you are pressurising the participants.

- Emphasize the common goal.

- From 'you' to 'we'. A speech that uses 'you' leading on to 'we' stresses the feeling that 'we belong together'.

- Apply the initial benefit promise (IBP) from the beginning and emphasize it continuously.

- Make acceptance easier by making it attractive from the listeners' point of view.

Tactical tips

1 Analyse the motivation of the target group

A Attitude	1 negative	2 neutral	3 positive
B Interest	1 low	2 medium	3 great

In the case of A1 and B1 you will have great difficulties succeeding with a persuasive speech. A2 and B2 are feasible. In the case of A3 and B3, don't attempt to give a persuasion speech – they're already convinced. Of course, there are other variations on this. Only if you really know who you have in front of you, can now communicate successfully – that is deliver a custom-made presentation.

2 To win over, not overcome your target group

An example: Several of your members of staff have been headhunted by a competitor. You want to keep them, so you have to convince them to stay. If you purely talk them into staying, steamroller over their arguments, criticize them as being disloyal or even call them deserters and, effectively, silence them, rather than persuade them, you will most certainly lose your members of staff, either immediately or at a later date. If you prove to your political opponents that their position is logically untenable, you won't win them over. If you explain to a customer group that accepting a certain offer from your competitor would be a costly mistake, the order will go, at best, to an uninvolved third party. *You cannot persuade someone against their will.*

3 Finding common denominators

Which aims do you and your opposite numbers have in common? Emphasize those points to the maximum. Maybe you need some compromise solutions to do this. There must be a mutual benefit – a win–win solution.

4 Use the word 'you' continually

If you want to win people over (as opposed to overcoming them), dissipate resistance and change opinions. You have to appeal to the participants' self-interest.

5 Show an understanding attitude to conflicting opinions

'You are right' wins more people than 'you are wrong'.

6 Place one negative point between two positive ones

'You have better chances of promotion with our company. You say that the other firm has offered you a higher salary, yet we can offer you a new, spectacular profitsharing scheme'. You sandwich your offer (plus, minus, plus).

7 Think about the significance of winning their favour

If you are liked, you have already won half the battle. If not, you won't be able to persuade, however good your arguments are.

8 *Look for support from allies*

References, examples and evidence taken from their experience, witnesses, opinion leaders

9 *Important: use AP constantly*

Ask for agreement point by point: 'Is that OK? Do you see it this way, too? Can you agree with this? Can we consider this point as being settled?'

Some more tips for success

Is it sensible to show your cards at the very start of a persuasion speech or should you leave that to the end? If you want to win others over with your persuasive speech, you first of all have to open their minds to what you are about to say. For example, there is a choice between two candidates for the post of sales manager. Some of the members of the Board favour Mr Smith, whereas you are for Mr Brown. If you say immediately, 'I am for Mr Brown because ...', you run the risk of your opponents – that is, the advocates of Mr Smith – not even listening to you any more. You won't arouse curiosity, just resistance and possibly even antipathy. Or – and this is just as dangerous – your opponents concentrate on finding weak points in your statements. On the other hand, if you start off by saying, 'Mr Smith or Mr Brown, that really is a difficult decision as there are arguments in favour of Mr Smith, but also in favour of Mr Brown ...'. With such an opening phrase, you make the participants curious to hear what you are going to say. You achieve open communication.

> **If you want to persuade, don't let the cat out of the bag immediately!**

It is different, however, in the case of a debate (see Chapter 13), a panel discussion, an experts' forum or an unfriendly debate, where the participants' views are very contrary to each other. There you are under time pressure and often have to 'show your cards' immediately to get a chance to speak at all and to stand out. Who first occupies the scene generally wins.

Special tip: Use the formula (DIPADA) to structure a persuasion speech

The following six key words will help you to structure your persuasion speech. Remember the DIPADA formula and practise the six-step structure several times using different cases.

1 Define Not your own opinion, but the desires, attitudes, aims and needs of the people you are addressing. First of all, you need to know what they want. Say silently to yourself, or even openly, 'you want...', followed by the AP: 'is that correct?'

2 Identify With your suggestion, your solution. This means achieving agreement on it: 'You want ... There is a solution to this. Could it look like this?'

3 Prove Proof of point 2 – the correctness of the identification. 'Are these tips and this evidence convincing?'

4 Acceptance Give the participants a chance to accept your proof; get their agreement in the form of consenting AP: 'This would mean the following conclusion ... Is that right?' The participants answering 'yes' openly or by nodding, say, is your AP signal.

5 create Desire Arouse desires in your participants. Your suggestion should not only appear plausible, it should have some emotional appeal. 'We' alone is not enough, *everyone* must feel addressed and appealed to. People must desire a solution, not only accept it with their brains.

6 Agreement Your conclusion summarizes the six steps and gains agreement, at least in principle.

MOTIVATION SPEECHES

Occasions

Preludes to campaigns, cooperation, demonstrations, to activate people, defuse a crisis.

Target group's attitude

Supporters – positive.

Aim

Stimulate, motivate, fire up, inspire.

> **Bear in mind that logic does not create enthusiasm.**

Techniques

- **Emotional appeal** 'The spark has to spread quickly'. Emotions create emotions. If there is no spark, there is no ignition. Logic doesn't create enthusiasm.

- **Maximum impact** To be able to carry others along, your voice, language, drive, determination and the strength of your conviction must all combine to create a powerful impact. You should only give such a speech if you are yourself totally convinced.

- **'We', 'together'** This is a pure 'we' speech. 'You' separates you from the participants. Carefully analyse the target group's motivation first of all! Is there any common ground?

- **Promise rewards** You cannot just make demands, you also have to be prepared to give something in return, such as the promise of success, the prospect of a reward, joy or pride in the performance achieved. Even Churchill, in the most famous of his speeches in 1940, promised, not only blood, toil, sweat and tears, but also 'victory' at the end of it all.

- **Emphasize the feeling of belonging together, of joint purpose**
  Are the participants really supporters? If you are addressing your own members of staff, for example, the fact that they are your employees alone does not mean a lot in itself. Many executives forget that fact. The determining factor is your goal. Is it going to be considered as being positive or negative from a subjective point of view? If the answer is 'No', you first have to give a persuasive speech.

If you are the manager of a football team and want to spur on your team before a crucial match, you don't have to find logical arguments to convince them. Rather, you motivate your players, reinforce the positive atmosphere and radiate your own commitment: 'We're going to do it boys. The whole town is with us.' You make a pep talk real. Or, 'We must and can reverse this downturn in orders. You have yourselves just worked out a way of achieving this. So, are we going to roll up our sleeves and get down to it? Our colleagues doubt our ability, but they did so last time as well. And we're going to show them again, aren't we?'

These techniques can also be applied to other situations in your everyday work. You may have to rally support and appeal to motivation at a work meeting or staff briefing. You can, for example, call on a few loyal colleagues you can rely on to support you at one or more points during your speech. Careful orchestration is also necessary during a motivation speech. If you are in the middle of an enthusiastic speech to your members of staff assembled for the occasion, at the end of which you want to solicit solidarity and, all of a sudden, the end of work siren goes off while you are launching your flamboyant appeal, you will probably have hardly any impact on the participants. Besides, they will have either already started to get up and leave or their thoughts will have wandered off on to subjects outside work. Maybe you should have given your speech earlier – or shortened it. Ridiculous mishaps, such as disturbing announcements on the public address system, or distorting sounds on the microphone can also turn a dynamic speech into a comic one.

Special tip

Use the following steps to structure a motivation speech.

1 Aim

'This is what we want' – say that right at the beginning. It has to be clear from your first sentence which stimulating goal you are trying to achieve. Let us look at an example of how to do this taken from a technology company. The Director of Research and Development is talking to the engineers about winning a large contract in the face of very stiff competition: 'We absolutely must get going to win the contract to supply the new equipment!'

2 Reward (or punishment)

'That's what's in it for us', is what you say. Only mention one, or, at the most, two tempting aims, without a lot of details: 'A better image, more money. That means, for us and for the company, that our jobs are guaranteed to be secure for months to come'. The negative (punishment)? Just reverse your promise of a reward.

3 Solution

'It is that simple.' Show only one of the possible ways to go – one that is easy for all the participants to follow – 'We just have to be quicker than the competition. By next Monday, the whole new proposal needs to be finalized'.

4 Ways

'This is the way we will proceed', brings you on to the next step. For example, 'We are now going to get our own suppliers cracking and build a prototype over the next three days and nights that we can demonstrate. The others won't be able to match that'.

5 Repeat the aim and reward

Remind your participants once more of your motivating goal and reiterate the prospect of the tempting reward again: 'We want to win this contract in order to secure all our jobs'.

6 Appeal, request, enthusiasm, agreement

'OK, let's go for it!' Now your spark has to light a fire in your participants. This is the moment of truth, have you done it or not: 'Right colleagues. Let's get cracking! OK? We'll win that order!'

ACTION SPEECHES

Occasions

Votes, decisions, commitments, resolutions, actions.

Target group's attitude

Supporters to 'followers' – very positive.

Aim

Triggering real, immediate action. That means specific, noticeable, controllable and immediate action. Otherwise, it remains a persuasive speech.

Techniques

1 Emotional and logical

Your arguments must be both emotionally *and* logically compelling. Structure the compelling, necessary and immediate action logically.

2 *Your charisma and power*

They should reach a crescendo. If your initial suggested idea is too strong right at the outset, this can easily characterize you as a fanatic and create a feeling of manipulation and cause resistance.

3 *Appeal to the 'we' feeling*

Complete identification of participants with the speaker and vice versa is a crucial condition for action.

4 *Step-by-step build-up*

This point is crucial for success. Stress every decision the participants agree to, step by step. This means that you have to divide the overall goal into sub-goals. For example, '... therefore, we have to do something, right?' (get agreement). 'It would be wrong to wait for a decision to come from the Commission, wouldn't it?' (get agreement). 'Therefore, we have to approach the public immediately, right?' (get agreement). 'This measure requires support from all members of the Board' (get agreement). 'This has to happen before the weekend, doesn't it?' (get agreement). 'So, do you all agree that I, on your behalf ...' (get agreement). Should you get a 'No' somewhere along the line, go back to the last 'Yes' before that and, if necessary, rephrase your argument. If you had made the suggestion in one big lump – 'Do you agree that ... all members ..., before ..., I ...' – and tried to get agreement, you would have possibly received a big, general 'No', killing your suggestion before it had had a chance. Understandable though, isn't it? Practise it to become familiar with the step-by-step approach. We know from all our international communication seminars that even very capable senior managers sometimes have difficulty putting the step-by-step structure, coupled with continual AP checks, into practice. So, cover yourself by asking for agreement from the participants for a decision at every stage along the way and then let your speech climax in an immediate controllable appeal for action, repeating, if necessary, the various yeses.

Tactical tips

As with all effect speeches, you have to make a careful analysis of your target group's motivation for action speeches, too. How important is the readiness of the participants to make a contribution? What is the minimum level of commitment you require? Don't go for more but insist on this. Now the crunch is whether you can manage to move the participants on from conviction to enthusiasm (or indignation) and then to (immediate) action. Bear in mind that the action *has* to be *immediate*, otherwise you'll give, at best, a persuasion speech (such as happened in one of the case studies at the beginning) and have no guarantee of success. Careful orchestration, again, is of crucial importance for an action speech. Everything has to be just right. To structure your speech, use the 'tunnel approach'.

Special guidance for structuring an action speech (the tunnel approach)

At the end of your speech, you want action. You want to get your participants to do something – to sign a petition, to stop or resume work, to go without one month's salary, to agree to a proposal from the Board to a budget plan, decide on a particular investment to buy premises, take over a company, to elect a Chairman or sack him, etc.

Imagine you are in a tunnel that is being flooded from behind you and you want to get out. Get the participants to visualize, and make them aware of, that same situation. Therefore, something has to be done. You place the participants in a tunnel and show them the exit at the other end. The way back has become impossible, you can't hang around any longer either and there are no other exits – the participants have no choice but to move forwards in order to escape the water pouring in and drowning them.

The steps of the tunnel approach are as follows.

1 Compelling solution (action is needed)

At the beginning, put the necessity to act (action, decision, agreement) first: 'We have to do something, otherwise we will be overtaken by events'.

2 Immediate actual action (has to start now)

Of course, you have to prove *why* it is essential to act immediately (for example, make an offer and limit the time they have to accept it, give it an expiry date, make it an emergency). You guide the participants through the tunnel: 'Today is the last day. If the press beats us to it on Monday, it will be too late. If we don't act now, we will soon have no choice and will be the villains'.

3 The carrot (brings a desired reward)

'This decision, to withdraw a successful product from the market even though its harmful side-effects have not yet been proven, will win us trust from the public and among our workforce – as well as giving us a clear conscience.'

4 Promise of success (it will work)

The underlying meaning that we will get out of the tunnel: 'If we withdraw the product in question immediately, there will be no campaign against us'.

5 Exclude other solutions (the only possible solution)

There is no other way out: 'Delaying tactics, holding on, getting experts' opinions, preliminary declarations and so on – we've considered them all, but they won't protect us from a campaign in the press and, therefore, present no solution'.

6 Eliminate negative consequences (the solution is definitely positive)

Create the feeling 'We will get through it alright'. 'The resulting costs and loss of profits of about £... can easily be absorbed, thanks to our excellent results'.

7 No way back (forwards is the only way)

Get the message across that the stage-by-stage decisions have already been made and the campaign has started: 'There is no going back. Six months ago we might have been able to take corrective steps, but, now, it is too late for that. The necessary instructions have already been pre-pared and, with your agreement, they can be put into effect at once. Time is running out. The bad news is already slipping out. We have burnt our boats'.

8 Based on real planning (thought through)

You can rely on us, everything has been well thought through. 'Here is the plan once more with the most important elements. Our experts have taken everything into consideration. You can rest assured'.

Note: You may not be able to manage all eight steps, due to circumstances. Use which you can, but at least steps 1, 2 and 4.

Get an immediate reaction

Now comes the appeal for a decision, the vote or signature. Your tunnel is in place. Here are a few tactical tips,

1 If the action involves the participation of the people present, give precise instructions: 'In front of you is a declaration for each of you. Please sign one of the two versions', or, 'Please raise your hands as a sign of acceptance'.

2 Initiate the action immediately after the decision has been made (bearing in mind the tendency of participants to delay, have second thoughts or postpone action): 'Joe, go and send a fax informing all the appropriate offices of our decision immediately'.

3 To solicit the smallest, simplest common denominator of an action,

involving the least risk, is a mandate (order) to you as the initiator. The more you ask of others, the greater the risk to you.

4 Each stage of the tunnel has to be proven. It is not enough to say, 'There is no other solution', you have to prove that this is so. Every unproven claim provides the basis for an 'anti-tunnel', that is, one that destroys your tunnel.

5 How to stage an anti-tunnel. An anti-tunnel is the conscious destruction of a tunnelled argument. You should master the construction of such an anti-tunnel as well. If you want to undermine a call for industrial action, for example, analyse the arguments in favour of the strike. Find the weak points, then select one or several tunnel elements that are the easiest for you to destroy. The speaker says, for example, 'We must act immediately.' You counter, 'Immediately? Why? Why must we? We can, but we don't have to'. Each delay reduces the likelihood of the tunnel being completed. Another example of how you can counter: 'Why can't we go back? Of course we can. We don't want to be steamrollered. Nothing is definite'. You don't necessarily have to give counter-evidence – doubts or alternative options may be sufficient.

6 Whether you call for an action or want to destroy it – using the tunnel or the anti-tunnel – you must yourself demonstrate your total commitment: Only with maximum commitment on your part will you succeed. Furthermore, the participants' AP is indispensable. Make use of the full range of your communication tools.

> **So, now you can answer the questions and solve the case studies at the beginning of this chapter!**

Always distinguish between the three categories of speech and decide which one is best suited to achieving your aim. Follow the simple formulas. Appeal to both emotion and logic. Motivate the participants, based on realistic judgement. Your aim is to win people over, not overcome them, in order to persuade or motivate them or trigger them into action.

11

HANDLING TRICKY QUESTIONS AND ATTACKS PROPERLY

Can you answer the following four questions?

1 **What is the overall impression when a very good speech is followed by a mediocre discussion?**

2 **Can you win participants over during a discussion by asking suitably worded counter-questions?**

3 **Should you agree with some friendly participants to help get a debate going?**

4 **Who should chair the discussion after your speech? You, the organizer or a professional moderator?**

Can you solve the following four problems?

1 At the annual shareholders' meeting of an energy generating company, two shareholders, sitting at the back of the room, repeatedly disrupt the discussion between the Chairman of the Board and another shareholder sitting in the front row by heckling. First of all, the Chairman asks the two hecklers to please be quiet and save their comments until later. However, they keep on heckling him. Finally, the Chairman asks them to leave the room, saying as he does so, 'I am exercising my right as Chairman of the proceedings.'

What do you think of this reaction? What would you have done in this situation?

_____

_____

_____

2 Chief executive David Guthmann is not used to anyone contradicting him in his German company as, to his 450 staff, he is a real entrepreneur. During a journey through the United States, he gives a speech about German economic policy to senior managers attending a seminar in Boston. During his speech, he is driven into a corner by questions that normally, he would have no problem answering. The discussion, held in English, is heating up and, suddenly, David can't find the right words. The unusual role and the surprising attacks make him overreact.

Could he have extricated himself from this situation by behaving differently?

_____

_____

_____

3 In a live debate on television, Chairman Gordon Chester proves to be a brilliant speaker during discussions of environmental issues. He has got an answer for every question, fends off every attack successfully with a convincing counter-argument and quick-wittedly counters all verbal interruptions. He presents his industry's point of view both proactively ('things we have achieved in the past') and reactively ('cost issues associated with the economic climate'). Gordon totally controls the debate.

How come he gains respect but is not liked?

_____

_____

_____

4 At a meeting of the local employers' association there is a discussion about whether or not to introduce weekend working as a temporary measure. Two camps emerge: some of the employers are strongly in favour of the suggestion, others strongly against it. John Miller, owner of a medium-sized company and actively involved in politics, says that there is no point at all in trying to convince people who hold a different opinion: 'As soon as I express my own view and show my cards the others will do the same, won't they? Both sides insist on being right without moving a jot. That's why it is pointless trying to have a discussion with your opponents, especially if they've committed themselves emotionally and rationally. That won't get us anywhere at all. The best thing is to have a vote immediately. It will also save us time'.

Is this attitude justified?

_____

_____

_____

TIPS FOR COPING WITH HECKLERS AND OTHER DISTURBANCES

Sooner or later it happens to every speaker: participants start disturbing the speech and make them lose their thread. One participant starts a conversation with the person next to them. Another one interrupts the speech, asking an unpleasant question, making a joke at the speaker's expense, contradicting repeatedly or even trying to prevent the speaker from continuing the speech. What would you do if something like this occurred during a speech of yours? Here are a few tips so you know what to do.

1 If you can answer convincingly, do so

Be fair, assertive and friendly. That is the best response to a disruption. If you can use a pun or an elegant parry, you will score a double victory. A politician was once interrupted during a debate on equal opportunities by a feminist: 'If I were your wife I would put poison in your coffee'. He responded tersely, 'If I were your husband I'd drink it'. The laughs were on his side and he managed to regain complete control of the debate.

2 Don't overreact

Standing on a platform on your own, it is very likely that you will feel a little exposed and so be oversensitive in the face of even harmless questions. You can *feel* as if you are under attack even when you're not. Everyone feels the same. Overreacting, of course, can lead to an escalation of the negativity, causing real damage. So, take a deep breath first, relax, control your emotions. Consciously play down the question or objection. You will notice that this will give you control of the situation once more.

3 Give them more

Interpret every objection, every unpleasant question, every attack as a request for further information and treat it as such. For example, if you are being attacked with the statement, 'You can't be serious about what you've just said!', you reply, 'What you have heard has not satisfied you. You would like to have better information, is that right? Let me try, OK?' When you get agreement, you can give this information – or just carry on asking further questions. Do this systematically. Interpret every attack as a request for more information. That way there will be no animosity. Did you notice that the reply contained three counter-questions? They give you control and three 'yes' answers, turning round the negative atmosphere that is created when you are attacked.

4 When in real difficulty

Use the strategy of consciously trying to gain time! It is better than coming out with the wrong thing or finding nothing to say at all due to irritation or panic. Postpone the question: 'Could you ask the question again a bit later?', or, 'Let's come back to that point later on'. Or, be frank: 'Let me think about that for a minute'. This last answer can even be taken as a compliment to the person who asked the question. The advantages of this strategy are that:

- you regain your composure
- you take the sting out of the discussion
- in the meantime, you can collect strategic plus points, for example by summarizing the points you and the participants have agreed on so far: 'We agreed on point a and point b. Point c, however, we'll have to have another look at. And as far as point d is concerned it looks like we agreed on ...'
- the point might clarify itself
- you also gain time if you ask the person concerned to repeat their question, explain it or give reasons for the question (or objection).

When *time* is won, almost *everything* is won!

- you involve other participants and turn the monologue or duel into communication (AP). You can ask:

- one specific person (expert)
- the whole group (the members can discuss the question among themselves)
- the person who asked the question in the first place (who will be delighted to show off)
- a volunteer ('Who would like to take this up?' or 'Who has a good answer?'). This route – the route of communication – will practically always help you out.

Use what you've got! You've got a microphone, the hecklers haven't! Speak assertively in a firm voice – that by itself will make the interruptions sound weak. You are standing in the limelight, the hecklers aren't. And don't forget: take a stand! Have courage to stick to your own viewpoint. Show your flag and mobilize your conviction and charisma. If you realize that you are about to weaken, make a short pause, take a deep breath, think briefly about something positive – and then articulate what you have got to say.

5 You can also isolate the disturber

If you have the feeling that the question probably does not interest the other participants or if you believe that the group feel that the heckler is being unpleasant, you can simply ask the group, 'Are all of you interested in this subject?' With this wording you run no risk. If there is no response – which is mostly the case – you have resolved the situation. If, however, two or three of the participants still raise their hands, you can say: 'OK, let's talk about it afterwards. Would you join me after my presentation?' Don't pause, otherwise the heckler will want to nail you there and then: 'No, I want an answer right now'. At any rate, your response should be both friendly and assertive. Show some tolerance: 'Never mind, afterwards we'll meet in the bar for a beer'.

6 Another possibility

A frequent mistake speakers make is to attack the heckler(s), and the situation turns into a duel. Instead, mobilize your allies! If you know that the majority is on your side, say, 'It is now 11.30. Shall we move on to the next point, ladies and gentlemen, so that we have finished by lunchtime?' Make sure, though, that you phrase your question so that you get a positive 'Yes' in reply. You have to win over the silent majority.

7 And yet another method

This is one media professionals use. Nobody, not even the trouble-maker who has just interrupted you, can speak longer than 12 to 15 seconds without having to breathe. Watch out for the moment when they stop to breathe. That is your chance. As soon as the troublemaker takes a breath, interrupt and do so quickly. Do it firmly, precisely at that moment and with a strong voice. Don't say, 'Excuse me for interrupting you'. You risk the heckler replying, 'No I won't – don't interrupt me!' A good peg to hang your interruption on is the phrase, 'In this context, Mr Smith ...' , or even, 'Right, now let's ...'. You needn't worry that you will make a bad impression on the other participants by doing that. On the contrary, if you, on their behalf, tackle the trouble-maker with their own weapons, you are likely to earn the participants' admiration, and you also regain complete control of the situation.

8 A simple method

To get the upper hand with the troublemaker, use the following tech-nique, one that is used only too rarely. Yet, it is not only elegant but also extremely successful. Ask the heckler to come up on to the plat-form. In most cases, hecklers sit in the last row, surrounded by their own people. That's where they feel strong. And you have to get them out of there. So, you first of all ask, 'What was your name again?' When the heckler replies, you say, 'I can't hear you!' The heckler says their name again, a bit louder. Now you move on. 'Right, Mr Selfman, please come up here to the platform, we'll be able to hear you better then'. Now the heckler has two options. First, to chicken out. That brings you on the road to victory and you can say, 'But we can hardly hear you. That's a shame, what you wanted to say was probably important. Can we see each other briefly afterwards?' Second, to come to the front. All the better. In this case, too, there is hardly any danger for you any more. The moment they leave their own territory and enter your 'arena', the platform, they are in your hands. Be polite and welcoming, saying 'May I show you how the microphone works? Like that, that's right, not too high, and take care not to knock it, otherwise you'll deafen us all. How much time will you need? Just tell us briefly who you are before you begin'. Such a friendly introduction tames even the most irate heckler. You are the ringmaster, the heckler is in the weaker position, so go out of your way to appear helpful. Even if they only want to talk for two or three minutes, give them five. They probably won't be able to fill that time without boring the participants. Always show a friendly face meanwhile. And – very important – don't try to ridicule the heckler! Otherwise, the participants will take their side and think you are being arrogant.

> **Taking a deep breath calms you down!**

9 Don't forget TMM

This stands for tell me more! Don't just let the person concerned finish what they are saying, encourage them to say even more: 'I'm sure you have some further thoughts on that subject', or, 'What prompted you to make that statement?' or just, 'could you expand on that?' Then they have to talk, more than they'd probably like to. That way you make the heckler run dry. The more they talk, the more scope for counter-attack they offer you, and the heckler certainly won't have bargained for that.

10 Counter-questions and the boomerang approach

If you respond to an interruption by asking a counter-question, you regain the initiative. It is your move again. You don't defend yourself, you are on the offensive. Remember, in communication, the offensive always wins over the defensive! The counter-question can be factual, but also personal: 'How come you, of all people, ...'. The third type of counter-question is the boomerang question. It has another, more far-reaching function. It is designed to clarify which answer or piece of information would satisfy your opponent. This question – 'What would satisfy you?', or 'Which point can we agree on?', or, 'Where do you see the solution yourself?' or, as a key principle, 'What answer (proof, information etc.) would satisfy you?' – must be asked before giving your answer. That way, you don't strain your imagination unnecessarily, you tie your opposite number down and control the situation.

11 Another hint on how to deal successfully with attacks

Think of an iceberg: by far the larger part of it is beneath the water's surface and so can't be seen. Now think of this in human terms: at the top is logic, at the bottom is the emotions. In a discussion or a debate, you can communicate on two different levels: the intellectual level of the mind and logic, and on the invisible – yet far more dangerous level of emotions and feelings. If you are attacked on the intellectual level, your answer has also to be directed by the mind. Should you be attacked on the emotional level, however, fight back with emotional points. What you mustn't do, though, is attempt the so-called 'crossed communication'. It is dangerous and pointless. For example, you are attacked with rational, sober arguments and you react irately and emotionally: 'How dare you accuse me of misrepresentation?!' A dangerous mistake. Your opponent will ask you coolly and forcefully to respond to their factual objection with a factual argument. If you don't, you will soon be beaten – the opponent will show you up in front of the whole group, winning with their calm, logical arguments. The other way round is just as fatal. You are being attacked on the emotional level but react with a logical answer. The attacker indignantly shouts across the room: 'You are a charlatan. You are manipulating the figures, you are! How dare you make such assertions?' You, as the attacked, try to stay cool and say, 'May I explain these points one by one again to make sure there are no misunderstandings? In addition I would like to add the following research results that prove ...'. No, this is not a good idea. You will not come across well. A better reply would be, 'Mr Mad, I can understand if you are outraged by this. I would be too, if it was really the way you think it is. But that is not the case. I am not manipulating them and, indeed, am saddened by your assertions'. This is an emotional reaction to an emotional attack. Then, depending on the reaction, the discussion should either be continued on the logical level, or possibly, go on to an emotional level. If you take this method to heart and master it, you will survive many nasty debates.

> **Always communicate on the same level! Match emotion with emotion, reason with reason.**

12 Our experience from international communication seminars shows time and time again that you must practise!

Understanding and applying aren't the same thing. That's why practice is needed. If you are frequently confronted with disruptions and attacks, you should practise how to react when under fire. We all know what a problem icy roads are in winter. Most of the year we drive on clear roads, then, all of a sudden, we hit an icy spot one morning and react in the wrong way. If we practised on a skid pan at a training school, however, we would be well prepared for the real thing. The same applies to communication. It is not enough to read this chapter and *imagine* a disruption happening. Get a group of friends together and let them attack you repeatedly to practise how to react. That's how you train for the real thing. You will notice how much better you are. You deal increasingly successfully with disruptions.

Don't let the large amount of space that has been dedicated to dealing with disturbances here give you the impression that these occur frequently during presentations. The vast majority of questions, objections and comments are fair and positive (even if you don't always think so) with just a hint of ego in the background. But, as with safety, take no chances. Enough of how to behave in the face of attacks and disruptions during a speech! Let's now move on to how to use the time *after* the speech. A speech is often followed by a discussion. Remember:

> **An excellent speech is often completely ruined by the speaker's bad performance in the discussion afterwards.**

TIPS FOR HANDLING DISCUSSIONS

1 Leave the platform at the end of your speech

At the end of a speech that went down well, you will often be warmly applauded by the participants. Worried about what to do? Don't be! Should you bow? Never! Say 'thank you'? Again, never! After all, you are not an actor or a musician. For an artist, their performance is their purpose. For you, however, your speech is only a means to an end. Therefore, leave the platform – without any special gestures. You will still get your applause. Take your notes discreetly with you or have someone collect them for you later. What you have used up there to help you during the speech is no one's business.

2 Only speak again during and after a discussion (or questions)

Resist the temptation to add more things after your speech – even if something important should suddenly spring to mind or you have forgotten to mention a major point. Better luck next time. You know from the programme there is going to be a discussion after your speech so get ready for it. And here is an important strategic rule: Never finish the event with the discussion. Having a discussion at the end brings with it considerable risks:

- it can go wrong, through no fault of your own

- you have no opportunity to put things straight again

- it can end on a sour note

- you are no longer centre stage.

Rather, have the sequence of events announced in the following way: 'After the presentation, there will be a discussion from ... until ..., followed by a brief summary and overview by the speaker'. This, of course, means that you need to have *two* speech conclusions: one to finish your speech proper and one for the conclusion after the discussion. You can plan the first ending precisely, the second one, though, only in part as you won't know which points will be covered in the discussion and how it will go. Therefore, structure your second close in a way that allows you to adapt it to the course of events. You can straighten points out, explain them or build on them. Make sure it is always you who has the last word. Your final word leaves the last and lasting impression. Make it powerful, mobilize your skills for projecting your message.

3 Determine your goal for the discussion

And plan accordingly. What is the purpose of the discussion? Reinforcing? Giving additional information? Having opinions from all sides discussed in detail, even opposing ones? Strengthening the impact? Is it purely a formality? Other aims are often revealed in the wording of the programme, in such phrases as 'An exchange of ideas', or 'Working out new approaches', or, 'Clarifying additional points'. Each of these requires a different approach. You, as the speaker, have great interest in influencing the character of the discussion that follows your speech.

4 Organize it properly

Announce the rules of the game and get them accepted. Influence the choice of chairperson. Stage-manage it. Everything should be angled towards your goal (see point 3 above). Who do you think should chair the discussion? You have three options: the organizer of the event, a professional moderator or yourself. The most risky solution is often choosing the moderator as they are mainly paid to make the discussion exciting. In order to create suspense, a professional moderator might heat up the atmosphere. That can easily be done at your expense. Their own ego can make them turn against the speaker, contradicting, provoking and even teasing the speaker, eroding their composure, all of which will make the moderator look good. Tip: do whatever you can to meet the moderator before the discussion and win them over to your side. Make the moderator your ally, if you can't avoid the person or they are really good. A fact that speaks in favour of choosing the organizer of the event to chair the discussion is that they wish you no harm, as they want the event to be successful. The disadvantage is that they are often not a professional. They may want to demonstrate their own knowledge. The best solution is for you to handle the discussion yourself. You can then direct the discussion in whichever way you want. You then also don't have to place the discussion at the end of your speech at all – you can simply integrate it into your presentation. This means you'll also automatically have the final word. This solution carries the least risk for you!

As the chair, announce the rules of play and secure the participants' agreement by asking approval for your rules: 'How long do we want this discussion to last? Half an hour? Agreed? Therefore please keep your questions as short as possible, at the most one minute. My answers should take no longer than two minutes. Agreed?' Once the rules have been laid down, they stay in force until the very end of the event – and they apply to everyone! Stage-manage the discussion, including the overall structure, sequence and direction, as well as the organization. Watch out for raised hands, don't overlook anyone. The first question decides on what level discussion will take place. Therefore, if possible, have the first questions prepared in advance. Alternatively, you can throw in the first question.

5 Once again

Always consider and treat comments or objections as requests for clarification. As mentioned earlier, when standing on a platform or chairing an event, it is easy to overreact to anything that even remotely smells of criticism. You don't believe it? It is true – although most questions are not criticisms, but misunderstandings or unclear points or ego trips. Have a positive attitude yourself! It will give you the necessary composure.

6 Create a pleasant atmosphere

Express in a positive way what is not absolutely negative. Don't say, 'This is wrong', say, 'The following is true ...' instead. Appear friendly, even if it's hard. Praise the participants' comments, whether they are objections or questions, say, 'This is a very good point you're making'. This channels the participants' desire for an ego trip in the proper direction. Don't let duels develop. Instead, involve everyone, if possible: 'Ask your neighbour what they think about this'. If necessary, protect the person who asks trite or silly questions or makes tedious comments. Raise the value of these statements. This earns you plus points and encourages others to participate as well.

Several of the pieces of advice are equally applicable to debates where you have been invited to represent a certain position. You are sitting there together with other representatives who hold differing opinions – industrialists, environmentalists, employers, trade unionists, conservatives, left-wing politicians, directors of personnel, fundamentalists, members of the establishment, non-conformists etc. – what do you do? Read the tips below, practise them and use them next time this happens to you!

HOW TO PERFORM CONFIDENTLY IN A DEBATE – AND PERSUADE PEOPLE

1 Start in advance, research attitudes

Do your homework before the debate. Establish the opinions the other participants have on the subject to be debated. In doing this, you know the various camps right from the start of the event. Think who your opponents are, who your allies are? Which view will receive the most support? To what extent can you influence your opponents individually beforehand? How do you stay in tune with your allies? This coordination is very important and should be done in detail to make sure that you don't all 'feather your own nests'.

2 Analyse the subject carefully

What are we going to debate? What lies behind the subject? Is it in your interest to interpret it widely or narrowly? Write these points down, by all means. There are debates where the participants talk until they're blue in the face about anything under the sun, but not about the original subject. Like the Directors of a publishing house, who, at a Board meeting, were supposed to discuss the following subject on their agenda: 'How to avoid the negative effects of our credit control policy'. After half an hour, the participants were debating whether unsolicited sales calls to large customers were appropriate or not. That can happen very quickly and the debate then often gets out of hand and becomes a pursuit of the trivial.

3 Concentrate on a few arguments and on the real subject

Two or three good arguments are more successful than listing eight or ten arguments. Worse still, if eight participants from your own 'faction' present eight different ideas. The few arguments must be presented with power and conviction. Good arguments can also be repeated several times or given more weight by means of examples.

4 Adopt roles, listen, adapt statements, interrupt

If several members from one group, one company Board, one organization or one political party participate in the same debate, each individual should be assigned a role. This is best done at the pre-debate rehearsal meeting of the group. Some members will restrict themselves to listening, others to responding specifically to opponents' arguments, while others can note arguments and new ideas down and, if appropriate, pass them over to those who are actively debating. If all your participants concentrate on their own verbal contributions to the debate no one will listen attentively to what the others are saying and you will miss many opportunities. Equally, no debate goes exactly according to plan and, therefore, you have to adapt your comments. The statement 'What I really wanted to say is something that has now already been covered, but I still would like to re-stress it briefly', is utter nonsense! Things that have passed in a debate are over!

If a debate gets bogged down or is in danger of escalating, a break can have a miraculous effect. Have the courage to interrupt and ask for a ten-minute break. This will allow everyone to get out of the clinch, take a breather, gather new ideas and retune your allies' thoughts. Such a break also usually improves the general atmosphere, yet this opportunity is rarely used.

5 Don't show your flag too early

Voicing your definite opinion too early during the debate makes you more prone to attacks from your opponents. Having to back out is always unpleasant. An opening statement like: 'I am in favour of solution Z, because...', won't help you win a single opponent on to your side. People will just search for a clever reply. And yet, you can constantly hear this kind of thing being said during debates. It is better to let others have their say first. Of course, when tempers have risen high in the debate, the subject is being hotly debated and it is difficult to get a word in, *then* is the time to become very direct and say, 'Now is the time to make it absolutely clear ...'.

6 Strong start, strong close; attack weak points, defend strong ones

To recall the conclusions of Chapters 6 and 7, strong opening, strong close. The first sentence is the second most important, the last sentence the most important one. The same applies to each of your individual contributions to a debate. This is why you should think carefully beforehand which sentence you want to use to begin your statement and what you are going to say to conclude it. Listen carefully to what the others are saying. Which of their arguments was the least convincing? Where is the weak point in their evidence? Where are the gaps? It obviously makes more sense to attack your opponent's weak points, rather than their strong ones. If you are attacked, retreat to your strongest arguments. Often, powerful answers count more than logical ones. These are easier to defend and can earn you plus points.

7 Use audio-visual aids and AP

Re-read Chapters 2 and 5. The use of audio-visual aids and active participation of the participants does not only make sense in speeches, it makes sense in debates, too. American politicians (Reagan, Perot, Clinton) are good examples of how effective this is.

8 Grasp every common denominator and look for them

As soon as you spot a common denominator – no matter how small it is – use it to build a bridge to your opponents. No one is ever 100 per cent right nor 100 per cent wrong. Go into each debate with a positive attitude and don't insinuate bad intentions on the part of others. Go to great lengths to interpret even negative statements positively. And, when you hear one of your opponents say something that largely corresponds with your own opinion, then tell them so. This reduces unnecessary tension and brings you closer to a joint solution. Praise builds support and disarms. And now think for a minute: when was the last time you heard a politician or others in a debate or an opponent say, 'You are right!' – and without using '... but' afterwards? How often do you hear instead, 'You are mistaken (or you are wrong), because ...'? When was the last time *you* said, 'You are right'? Debates fought like battles are not communication.

9 Avoid isolated statements

Gather allies. Say 'we', not 'I'. It is important in a debate to win massive support for your own position. If you isolate yourself with what you are saying you will lack the allies you need. So, say 'we' instead of 'I'. Don't let yourself be separated and beaten one by one. It is difficult for an opponent in a debate to argue against a whole group.

10 Make any concessions only at the last minute; set a high initial goal and don't be too 'reasonable'

If you make concessions very early during the debate, you run the risk of the other participants thinking that you give in easily. Consequently they will make even more demands. It is better to set yourself a high initial goal and then give in a *little*. This gives the impression that you are willing to compromise and allow the others to feel they have achieved something.

To summarize:

- **prepare with particular care**

- **don't aim for tactical 'successes' at the expense of your strategy**

- **being logically right is not the same as being emotionally acceptable**

- **don't lose track of your overall goal**

- **consensus is better than dispute!**

Discussions are sometimes more crucial to the overall impact you make than the presentation itself. The best speech can be destroyed by a bad discussion, Practise the rules for discussions, then you will be able to persuade people – by successfully communicating with them.

> Can you now answer the four introductory questions and solve the four case studies at the beginning of this chapter?

12

ABOVE ALL, MOTIVATE!

Can you answer the following four questions?

1 Why are motivation and communication inseparable?

2 Do all people have the same basic motives for action?

3 Are the motivations of a group the same as the sum of the individual motivations of the group members?

4 To what extent are there dominating motives in people, which are comparatively easy to spot?

Can you solve the following four problems?

1 Arthur Sullivan, the new Sales Director of an important mechanical engineering firm, speaks in front of departmental managers, the sales office staff, his sales force and representatives from abroad about the company's future. He is dynamic, full of daring ideas, enthusiastic and sharp in his presentation (sometimes even antagonizing the listeners unintentionally). His previous experience with fast-moving consumer goods companies is obvious and irritates some of the participants. His successes are met with resentment in some quarters. Many don't forget some of his comments, such as: 'What we need is a breath of fresh air .... some new blood', 'a clean sweep with a new broom ...', 'give the young ones a chance'. His brilliant presentation culminates in an appeal for 'more commitment, insight and determination in order to achieve the company's objectives and also more willingness to take risks and to dare to come up with new ideas'.

The response is reserved, and Arthur tries to hide his disappointment. Has he done something wrong? Chosen the wrong tone? Ignored the company culture?

_____

_____

_____

_____

_____

2 A small firm that produces screws is in a difficult situation. The traditionally run company, with 40 mostly older employees, who have worked for the company for decades, has been in the red for 2 years. The reasons are a decline in incoming orders, old manufacturing equipment and low productivity. The situation can't be expected to improve in the short term. The owner of the company, Benjamin Richter, is faced with two options: he can either close down the company and retire or make ten members of staff redundant and streamline the company. He decides in favour of the second option. Ben calls a staff meeting and confronts his colleagues with the depressing facts. Having presented all the figures and painted the future in a not too rosy a light, he tells the assembly of his decision to make ten colleagues redundant at the end of the next quarter. Of course, he expresses his regret and reassures his staff that times will get better again. The speech has a catastrophic effect. None of the staff feels involved or motivated. Instead, all of them are worried and depressed. Consequently, even in the months after the staff meeting, there is no increased drive among the staff, no one makes particular efforts and productivity keeps on declining.

How could Benjamin have drastically changed course from the point of view of communication?

_____

_____

_____

_____

3 A controversy breaks out at the Board meeting of a large management consultancy. Some Board members would like to spend more energy on winning new clients, whereas others think it more important to cultivate, deepen and extend existing client contacts. Over the last few months, a number of longstanding customers have ended their relationship with the firm, apparently out of dissatisfaction with the firm's performance. Jim Fernandez, the first to speak at the meeting, argues in favour of the second option. He says, 'I would like to plead for trying first to satisfy our existing clients, as a respectable firm should, and secure our position against attacks from our competitors before even attempting new goals'.

He only gets agreement to his speech from his allies. He did argue convincingly, but he forgot something. What did he forget?

_____

_____

_____

4 The candidates from two parties present themselves to their constituents in a small village during an election campaign. They each have only five minutes to speaк. After the first one has spoken and presented mainly the party principles, described its achievements and appealed to the audience for trust and support, the second speaker gets up to talk: 'Do you want to have more money in your pocket at the end of the month, without worrying that the taxman will take most of it away from you again? Would you like to see a stronger agricultural industry, which many of us earn our livelihood from? Be able to afford a holiday more often and be able to enjoy life a little more? You have the chance. These are not illusions. Each and every one of us can be better off next year'.

To which one of the politicians will the people prefer to listen? Even if they possibly have a sceptical attitude towards the promises made? The speaker who wins the participants' attention also has a chance to change their opinion. There are solutions to this. Do you know them?

_____

_____

_____

_____

THE ART OF COMMUNICATION

The art of communication lies in establishing a genuine relationship with the participants. This is achieved by appealing to the motivations of the target group. Many a politician, company or club chairperson have asked themselves, 'Why does what I am saying not go down well?' The answer, often, is because motivation is unknown to them.

> If you are unable to, first, motivate your participants to listen to you and, second, appeal to their basic motivations, those that make them tick – your speeches will only earn you a yawn.

Nine out of ten information speeches make no impact because the speaker has not appealed to the target group's motivations. Instruction speeches make no impact because the participants have not been motivated to learn. Pep talks fail because the speaker is incapable of arousing motivating emotions. Speeches to employees put them off instead of attracting them. Presentations to customers are phrased egocentrically and so miss the potential motives that would close deals. Company owners misread the common denominators between their own aims and those of their staff and talk over their heads. Older people want to instruct and educate younger ones (who neither want to be instructed nor educated) and younger people tell older people that times have changed, which thought, of course, is instantly rejected. The four case studies are further examples of this lack of connection.

So, what are the motivations or primary drives you can appeal to? There are more than you can fit into any one speech. Just have a look at the following list. It is detailed, but by no means complete.

SOME PRIMARY MOTIVES THAT CAN BE APPEALED TO

Ego

- prestige
- importance
- ambition
- vanity
- self-confidence

- power
- recognition
- esteem
- exclusiveness
- distinction

- praise
- status
- individuality
- title
- career

- success
- respect
- performance
- progress
- competition
- victory
- promotion
- Pride
- superiority.

Security

- property
- reliability
- assurance
- stability
- defence
- protection
- insurance
- guarantee
- trust
- help
- proof
- solidity.

Curiosity

- discovery
- play
- search
- experience
- research
- interest
- experiment
- development
- secret
- question
- revolution
- knowledge

Contact

- group
- joining
- belonging
- helping
- togetherness
- link
- cooperation
- warmth
- friendship
- relationship
- friendliness
- popularity.

Monetary gain

- income
- revenue
- capital
- economy
- property
- money
- investment
- earnings
- shares
- savings
- profit
- wealth.

Love

- sex appeal
- affection
- masculinity

- attraction
- seduction
- eroticism

- fascination
- flirtation
- charm

- femininity
- tenderness
- desire.

Comfort

- ease
- quiet
- release
- simplification

- rest
- inertia
- relaxation
- relief

- well-being
- amenity
- care
- idleness.

Health

- holidays
- sport
- play
- way of life

- lifestyle
- food
- medicine
- exercise

- relaxation
- recovery
- cure
- prevention of illness.

Of course not everyone responds to appeals or motivations in the same way, so you have to differentiate. Neither can you determine the motivation of a whole group by simply adding together the individual motivations of its members. Instead, you should take the mean of the motivations of the dominant members of the group and weigh up the preferences to get rid of extreme attitudes.

Use the P/S structure as a useful, simplified, practical key for determining motivation. It covers about two thirds of all motivational appeal situations you will find in your professional and private life. It covers most of your communication issues. P stands for power (or ego), S for security (or protection). There are three possibilities.

1 **Strong P, weak S** Your opposite number has a very strong urge for *power*. In that case, their need for security is low on their list of priorities, so they will respond strongly to the prospect of winning P (and also losing it), but not to any S appeals.

2 **Strong S, weak P** This person has a great need for *security*, which means that their quest for power is not very marked. Therefore, you can appeal to their S, but not to P.

3 **Average P, average S** Power and security are balanced. That means, however, that both motivations are only moderately present. You can appeal to both P and S, but with limited effect.

To express it in a matrix:

1	P (strong)	s (weak)
2	p (weak)	S (strong)
3	p (average)	s (average)

Have a look at the list of primary motivations. Take the first and second entries (power and security), then add the third (curiosity) to the first and the fourth (contact) to the second. Now take ten people you know and you'll find that you can easily put them into one of the three P/S categories.

If you address a group where the power drive is dominant and use words emphasizing aims such as power, prestige, recognition and praise, then you will have found the right approach. If you appeal to security, however, talk of caution, assurance, consolidation and support, you will not be warmly applauded.

Talk to a group where the desire for security is prevalent with such phrases as: 'We're really going to go for it now – it's all or nothing', or, 'We can afford to take risks', or, 'We'll get there against all odds', or, 'We're going to show them', and you will see a fair few sour faces.

When you are presented with a mixed group – where P and S are equally strong – it is true that you can hardly go wrong, but you won't cause a wave of enthusiasm with your arguments either. The very word 'group' denotes people who have something in common, otherwise you cannot appeal to them *as a group*. Of course, it is easier to appeal to the motivations of one individual person, and that is why, in difficult cases, one-to-one conversations are more likely to be successful.

Every benefit promise, every suggestion put forward must appeal to the listeners' motivation. Don't think that only material promises work. Success, pride, performance, loyalty, affection, sacrifice are frequently stronger 'motivators'. Motivators create willingness to do something, to act, to perform. Lack of a reward, even a non-material one, will block people's willingness to perform.

This combination of communication and motivation is light years on from applying pure rhetoric. Rhetoric is only a polished presentation. *Communication* turns *listeners* into *participants*. Of course, this involvement is more than a pure technicality, it requires genuine analysis and really taking note of the participants' motivations. It requires that you listen, which is more than just hearing or hearing someone out. Give others more opportunities to voice *their* views and what *you* say will also be listened to.

Should you feel the need to learn more about motivation, then have another look at *all* the previous chapters as motivation features substantially in each and every one of them. Without motivation, there is no communication. That is equally true of your own motivations, of course. You must feel motivated in order to be able to motivate others.

> The four questions and case studies at the beginning of the chapter won't give you any more headaches now.

Without motivation, there is no communication. If you want to persuade people, you have to be able to appeal to them, fulfil their primary needs and arouse positive emotions. Always bear in mind the two basic needs: power and security!

You have now learned how to win and persuade people. Use your skills well.

If you want to know more about communication, please contact:

Heinz Goldmann International Foundation for Executive
Communications
141, route de Chêne
CH–1224 Geneva

Tel:+41-22-348 4832 *Fax:* +41-22-348 4829

INDEX